Sell Well

To Vogue Salon & Spa – A Model of services retailing.

Bruce

WHAT REALLY MOVES
YOUR SHOPPERS

BRUCE D. SANDERS

ISBN: 1505540275
ISBN-13: 9781505540277
LCCN: 2014922294
Createspace Independent Publishing Platform,
North Charleston, South Carolina

CONTENTS

1

Where to Shop

〜9

In operating a retail business, your mission is to contradict a bit of old expertise from William & Mary College. Quite old expertise. In 1792, the proverb "Money can't buy happiness" made its first academically documented American print appearance. It was in *William & Mary College Quarterly*.

But as retailing professionals, we would like our shoppers to buy happiness from us.

Now, the nature of happiness differs among the consumers to whom we'll want to sell it. A principal distinction is between the instances in which people find happiness in excitement and instances in which they find happiness in calmness.

In all cases, the happiness consists of a sense of well-being. Still, we'll want to be ready to, first, determine which of the two types our shopper is looking for and, second, provide it. The difference impacts the type of products to feature. Positive excitement boosts shoppers' interest in products they can show off to others, but their interest in functional products—such as appliances unlikely to be seen by friends or family—doesn't increase nearly as much. When the shoppers' positive feelings consist of contentment and satisfaction with the ways things are now, their interest in functional products grows much more than does their interest in items with social esteem.

Compared to the calmness contingent, those looking for excitement tend to be younger and more focused on the future than on what's happening right now. In studies at University of Pennsylvania, Stanford University, and MIT,[1] subjects ages 18 to 25 preferred more stimulating choices than did those ages 50 to 58. The younger cohort selected "a refreshing peppermint blend" over "a relaxing blend of chamomile and mint," the bottle of "Pure Excitement" water labeled in bright orange over the "Pure Calm" one labeled in green, and the more upbeat version of the song "Such Great Heights."

Younger, future-focused consumers say they're happy when the store experience is exciting and enthusiastic. Older, here-and-now customers are happier when the store experience is calm, peaceful, and serene.

Yet, these are broad generalizations, and smart retailers attend to individual differences. Sometimes, it is the young who find happiness in calm. A while back, Ben & Jerry's ice cream shops introduced customers to a special selection of new flavors. With names like Chocolate Therapy, Apple-y Ever After, and The Last Straw, these flavors were not designed to stimulate. No, the Ben & Jerry's folks intended the new flavors to soothe.

Ben & Jerry's had gotten a bunch of input about what an entire sorority had named their "breakup ice cream brand of choice." The ice cream shops were ready to lift the spirits of their recently-dumped customers.

On the other hand, older consumers may be looking for excitement because that's what their younger consumption companions seek. These older consumers want to buy experiences which include family and friends. Here, the sense of well-being comes from spending money to share exciting times.

We know that having money, even temporarily, can insulate against unhappiness. Psychologists at University of Minnesota, Florida State University, and China's Sun Yat-Sen University[2] had one group of study participants count out eighty $100 bills. A matching group were assigned to count out eighty blank pieces of paper. All participants were then exposed to tasks in which they experienced social rejection and physical stress. The people who had worked with the $100 bills reported less discomfort during and after the tasks. Being in touch with the $8,000 gave people magical relief.

But as retailers, we'd prefer consumers to spend or deposit their money with us rather than count it. Because of the complex cross-currents and broad individual differences in consumer motivations, retailers can fail to spot some of the forces which move our shoppers to spend or deposit as they become customers, clients, or patients.

That failure to spot the forces is especially likely if a retailer is marketing to the mirror. When you assume your target customers hold the same preferences as you and make their purchase decisions the same way you do, that's marketing to the mirror.

People are much better at guessing what other people will dislike than at guessing what they'll like. Researchers at University of Michigan and McGill University[3] documented this with preferences in ice cream sundaes. People who liked a certain blend of ingredients—such as mint ice cream topped with hot fudge and sprinkled with walnuts—overestimated that others would like it by an average of 10%. Those who disliked the combination the experimenters had described overestimated others' dislike by an average of less than 1%.

Notice that in either direction, it was an overestimate, even if slight. Moreover, in making predictions of likes and dislikes, we tend to assume that other people come to their conclusions using reasoning similar to our own[4]. If they prefer Coke and we prefer Pepsi, we'll think they used the same criteria and weighting of criteria as we did in coming to our decision.

Let's apply this to your retailing tactics.

You might not spend time looking at circulars and discount coupons which arrive in your mailbox, but your prospective customers might. With running your store, you've less time to look at much of anything than does the typical shopper.

You might think your store's tag line is awfully clever and the store logo is a real grabber, but your prospective customers might not. You contemplated for long hours creating the tag line and logo, while shoppers have to comprehend the line and logo promptly or they'll move on.

Psychologists use the term "projection" to refer to the tendency we all have to assume that what we enjoy is embraced by those around us. In reality, this assumption can work for the very small retailer who is just getting the business started. The hobby shop owner and the purveyor of specialty foods can pay the bills for a little while by depending on a cadre of consumers who share the merchant's niche passion. This cadre knows about the store without having to read circulars, they're drawn even without discount coupons, and they can instantly decode the store's tag line and logo. This is because the cadre consists of the retailer's friends and family.

To grow the business, the retailer must broaden target markets beyond themselves. The flip side of projection is called "introjection." It consists of incorporating the perspectives of others into our own thinking, allowing the preferences and predilections of others to guide our actions.

It's harder for a retailer to engage in introjection than in projection. But it is incorporating the perspectives of others which can reveal the forces motivating purchases.

Beyond this, we might be overlooking powerful motivators because we forget that in consumer behavior, emotions trump logic.

A marketing researcher at University of Texas-Austin and forensic researcher at Northwestern University[5] asked study participants to say which of two automobiles they'd prefer. The only difference between the two cars was in the performance of the airbag in the car. Car 1 had an airbag that was more likely to save a life than was the airbag in Car 2. However, the airbag in Car 1 also had a small, but measurable, chance of causing death because of the force necessary to deploy the bag. The airbag in Car 2 had such a tiny probability of this happening that it wasn't even measurable.

Please stop for a moment and predict which of the cars your customers would choose. Is it Car 1, which is more likely to save a life in case of a crash? Is it Car 2, which you can count on not to kill you from deployment of the airbag? How is your prediction influenced by anything you know of the industry recall in 2014 of more than ten million vehicles containing airbags of a type implicated in deaths and injuries from exploding metal shards?

Are you ready to know what the research found so you can compare that to your prediction? Okay, then. In the study, more of the participants chose Car 2 than chose Car 1. They were placing greater importance on possibilities than on probabilities. Emotions trumped logic.

Chapter 1. Where to Shop

When it comes to weighing the risks, consumers tend to think in terms of possibilities—"How can I make this happen?" "How can I keep this from happening?"—more often than in terms of probabilities—"How likely is it that this will happen?" "How much would it cost me to make what I want twice as likely to happen?" "How much to make what I don't want half as likely?"

This occurs because thinking of possibilities is easier than weighing a set of probabilities. In making purchase decisions, shoppers use shortcuts. Otherwise the amount of information to process would be overwhelming, particularly when emotional decisions like life and death are involved.

The shopper is aiming to balance a whole set of risks, ranging from financial—"Is this price too high for what I should pay, too low to assure sufficient quality, or just right?"—to psychological—"How well do the personalities of this store and this product fit my values?"

As a general rule, keep it simple for your shoppers. Emphasize possibilities, not probabilities. This is what your customers want to hear. Notice how when state lotteries aim to build interest, they advertise bigger prize purses before advertising greater odds of winning any of the prizes.

People pay much more than justified by the odds in order to gamble on a lotto ticket. "You can't win if you don't play!" and "Somebody has to win!" become the rationales for spending money to turn a zero possibility of gain into a very small, but greater-than-zero, chance. People pay for an Extended Services Contract on an appliance even when the probability is that the cost of repair or replacement would be less than the cost of the ESC.

There are experts who look at this happening and conclude that shoppers are stupid. That's wrong. Sure, our customers sometimes make foolish choices. And we never want to exploit or mislead. But let's remember how the excitement from holding the lotto ticket and the peace of mind in having the ESC carry value.

Even when a retailer uses introjection and appreciates the influence of emotions in shopper psychology, that retailer could fail to appreciate the subtleties. Such as how numbers count.

I spent most of my elementary and middle school time living in Burbank and Hollywood, California, two centers of production of television shows and movies. Among my classmates were a few genuine child stars and a whole bunch of aspiring child stars, each of whom seemed to place great importance on the teacher getting their name right.

At the start of each school year, when the teacher would ask us to introduce ourselves, I found myself tickled by the special posture and tone with which each of the actual and potential child stars would announce their name. Pomposity, I'd call it, if I'd known what that word meant at my callow age.

My reaction to this was a bit of mischief: When it was my turn, I'd stand up, raise my chin so my eyes appeared to be looking down at the teacher, and spell it out. "B-R-U-the numeral 3-C-E. But the 3 is silent."

Consumer behavior findings indicate I was on to something. Numbers in names can add a special touch, and this is where I bring it back to improving retailer profitability. On your limited shelf space, which would you prefer to depend on to yield high sales: V8 juice or Campbell's tomato juice? Levi's 501's or Dockers?

Everything else being equal, a number in a product name will make it more attractive to your shoppers. V8 and 501's have an advantage over Campbell's tomato juice and Dockers. Still, there is an important exception to the appeal of numbers in product titles. Consistent with my name introduction experiment results, it has to do with movie stars—child and adult—or more accurately, with the movies they star in. Researchers at UCLA and University of Pennsylvania[6] found that, compared to numbered movie sequels, named sequels earn more box office receipts and receive better reviews. A numbered sequel seems to be too much like the predecessors— and may very well have been produced to achieve similarity with a proven formula. However, moviegoers usually prefer fresh experiences.

If the advertised benefit is novelty, not consistent quality, avoid sequential numerals.

The way in which you state numbers makes a difference, too. When deciding which measuring stick to use for the numbers, consider what fits your business ethics and how to best highlight selling points.

Larger numbers can make a benefit sound better. Researchers at Ghent University in Belgium and Tilburg University in the Netherlands[7] asked consumers to compare the advantages of a seven-year warranty and a nine-year warranty. To one group, the duration was stated as seven years compared to nine years. To another group, the identical durations were stated as 84 months compared to 108 months. Those consumers presented the months figures saw the difference between the warranties as larger than did the consumers hearing the comparison in years.

So numbers do count and there are subtleties to appreciate in the ways they do count.

The effect of cycles in consumer behavior sometimes masks the subtleties in how major motivators operate, such as with value and values—topics I'll discuss with you in the next two chapters.

During 2011, as Walmart Stores, Inc. was on its way to turning around eight successive quarters of declining same-store sales in the U.S., the company noticed that daily revenues during the first few days of each month were higher than daily sales during other days. Walmart attributed this to when paychecks were received and said it was evidence their customers were living paycheck to paycheck. Walmart changed their tactics to take full advantage of the cycle. They began to feature higher-priced merchandise at the start of each month.

Shoppers go through many sorts of cycles. It makes sense to cycle the merchandise to fit changing preferences. Before adapting this principle to your retailing business, consider a couple of points. First, your target demographic might be getting their paychecks weekly or biweekly rather than monthly. Within the monthly cycle, there could very well be smaller bumps at weekly intervals.

The second point to consider is that Walmart depends strongly on an image of everyday low prices on all items. The competitiveness of your business model may not depend that much on price. Do the paycheck cycles still make a difference in optimal merchandising techniques?

Yes, but from a different angle. Research at University of Utah and University of Iowa[8] finds that the effects are due to more than the consumer running out of money each interval. Paycheck cycles were found to affect not only how much money people will spend on merchandise, but also the types of merchandise they will find most attractive.

In the days soon after receiving a paycheck, consumers with full-time jobs become especially interested in products and services that would help them gain more than what they currently have. This is a time for you to feature the latest technologies and the toothpaste which promises to whiten teeth. Shoppers at these times also are more likely to spring for package deals. At the restaurant, one price for a salad/soup/appetizer, entrée, and dessert.

Then as the days after the paycheck pass, the person becomes progressively more interested in products and services which help them avoid losing what they have now. They'll pay greater attention to nostalgia items, familiar brands, and the cavity-fighter toothpaste. They'll avoid the package deals in favor of a traditional list of items under category headings.

There are biological cycles. Researchers at University of Minnesota, Texas Christian University, and University of Texas-Austin[9] found that women near the most fertile point of their monthly cycle are about 10% more likely to seek out sexier fashions than at other times of the month. When shopping for shoes, they'll lean toward the stilettos over pumps and toward revealing blouses over roomy sweaters. The evidence is that this cycle involves competitiveness. Among those females in the study told that attractive women frequented the neighborhood, things moved from 10% more likely to 25% more likely.

If you operate a ladies fashion boutique, note when each of your best customers expresses interest in particularly adventurous items and then, about one month later, contact the customer to offer items of equal adventure. The research findings indicate you'll sell well.

Supporting such findings in a less conventional service retailing venue was a research report titled "Ovulatory Cycle Effects on Tip Earnings by Lap Dancers," which occupied seven pages in the November 2007 issue of *Evolution and Human Behavior*. The study was conducted by three researchers from the University of New Mexico Department of Psychology.

Prior research had indicated that women near the most fertile point of their monthly cycle tend to be more attractive to males, as manifested in measures ranging from appealing body fragrance to selecting more fashionable clothing to enhanced verbal creativity. But does this make any difference in economic profitability?

Indeed it does, as least in the retailing situation examined by the researchers. With what I view as an adequate methodology for data collection and a very good methodology for statistical analyses, it was found that each dancer averaged $335 in tips per five-hour shift at the time of highest fertility. This was compared to averages of $185 and $260 per shift at the other measured points in the monthly cycle. The researchers' review of their own data plus that from prior studies showed no evidence that the dancers were conscious of the reasons for the differences in sales revenue.

Your customers—male and female—go through many sorts of cycles—biological and psychological—each day, each week, each month, each year. Knowing when to do what is essential to maximizing retailing profitability. Offering cold weather merchandise when your target consumers start thinking about cold weather preferences, for instance. Ordering the heavy sweaters and recruiting the tire chain jockeys enough in advance of when they'll be needed.

I don't know who first advised, "Timing is everything," but I do know that Tony Curtis, who appeared in more than 140 movies, is quoted as having said, "…(M)y longevity is due to my good timing." Albert Einstein associated time with the whole shebang since the Big Bang when he quipped, "The only reason for time is so that everything doesn't happen at once." Time your retailing practices to fit the cycles of your target audiences.

Then there are those areas in which consumer research findings flatly contradict generally-held beliefs about what sells well.

Probably for as long as retailing has existed, shoppers have been advised to make a list before entering the store. The shopping list protects against unwise impulsive purchases, it's said. With list in hand, the shopper can relax enough to have fun, knowing they'll get what they need, but not much more.

Well, it turns out that the value of the shopping list for the shopper depends on how the list is made. Researchers at Duke University, UCLA, and University of Florida[10] found that people who carry around the store shopping lists created from memory—the consumer trying to remember what they need and what the store carries—actually end up more likely to make purchases they will later regret.

Making a shopping list from memory uses mental energy. Every shopper has a limited pool of mental energy, and when a great deal of it is consumed in making the list, there is less mental energy left to resist the foolish, unhealthy, potentially sinful items.

How to have shopping lists work to benefit your customers? Encourage them to make what the researchers call "stimulus-based shopping lists," since stimulus-based lists require less mental energy. Give them the tools to look at what they have on their shelves and in the cabinets at home before coming to your store.

- In your advertising pieces, include a checklist the customer can use at home while surveying their supplies and then carry the list with them as they shop. Have copies of the checklist available in the store.

- Cook up recipes, suggesting combinations of foods or wardrobe items which fit well together. Prod the shopper to recognize that when they buy the beer, they'll want the chips and when they buy the paint, they'll want the primer. You'll serve as their memory.

- Be sure to include blank lines. This allows the customer to improvise beyond the rigidity of a list. Departing from the preplanning makes great sense for both you and the shopper when you are offering surprise in-store specials.

Stimulus-based shopping lists clarify communications, so help you recognize how your shoppers are achieving a sense of well-being and therefore the motivators to help you sell well.

Unclear communications fog that recognition. A single word can turn around your conclusions. One such word is "not."

"Never say never" is a fine inspirational motto because the self-contradiction in the phrasing reflects the incompleteness of most inspirational mottos. In that same spirit, I'll say "Do not use not," although the complete advice is less pithy: "Be aware that using 'not' when communicating with consumers often leads to misunderstandings."

Here's an illustration: Which toothpaste dispenser would receive higher ratings from your customers, the one you describe as "not easy to use" or the one you describe as "not difficult to use"?

Researchers at University of Colorado-Boulder, Northwestern University, and INSEAD[11] found that the "not easy to use" alternative received higher ratings.

Why? The answer has to do with how the two alternatives were presented: All the study participants were given one or the other of two versions of a list of characteristics of the toothpaste dispenser. The two versions were identical, except that one version included the "not easy to use" and the other, the "not difficult to use" phrase. The average ratings of liking were obtained for each separate group.

The participants had little trouble remembering what the phrasing said. It wasn't as if they failed to see the "not." Instead, it was that the "easy" or the "difficult" had much greater impact in the consumer's decision making than did the "not." One group was evaluating the toothpaste dispenser with "easy" in mind, while the other had "difficult" in mind.

The researchers found similar effects with a range of product categories. The use of "not" in item descriptions or usage instructions adds to the cognitive demands on the consumer, with the result that confusion is more likely. Consumers, especially older consumers, who were in a hurry when told that a product had "no added sugar" often remembered the product later as having added sugar.

To avoid confusion, omit "not." Or to use "not" to emphasize a contrast, employ "not this, but instead that." A druggist or physician could say, "Do not take this medication on an empty stomach. Instead, take this medication only right after eating."

Or I can say to you, as I will right now, "A failure to correctly understand a shopper's motivations can arise both from what you say and from what you do not say."

During a trip to train and consult with retailers in Modesto, California, I dined at a seafood restaurant in town. As those who have restaurant-hopped with me realize, I'm a two-napkin eater. I like to place one napkin on my lap and have the other at the ready on the table. Since buttery seafood can get messy, I hold out for two cloth napkins.

When my server—I'll call her Carolyn because that is not the name she used—brought the entree, I said, "May I have a second cloth napkin?"

She replied, "I can give you a paper napkin."

And I replied, "I'd like a cloth napkin. If it's a problem, please send the manager over. I'll ask him if I can have a cloth napkin."

And as Carolyn turned to walk away, she replied, "The manager is a woman."

Her last reply struck me as non sequitur silliness. What difference did it make if the manager was a man or a woman? In either case, please send over the manager so I can ask for a cloth napkin.

But as a psychologist and retail consultant, I was required to ask myself, "Why did Carolyn say that?"

The reason, I believe, is that she interpreted my "please send the manager over" as code words for, "Carolyn, you are incompetent. I need to go over your head to get proper service." She then fired back with her code words for, "You really have no business thinking I'm incompetent. You're not even able to wrap your head around the fact that a manager of a restaurant might be a woman. Where do you get off putting down women like you just did me?"

In reality, though, my words were code for, "I'll bet your manager told you that whenever a diner asks for an extra napkin, you should bring them a paper napkin so the restaurant can keep down costs. Therefore, if my request for a cloth napkin places you in a tough situation, Carolyn, let's please take you out of the middle of it by having me talk directly to your manager."

But I failed to say this, and by the time I realized my error, Carolyn had walked off. I used a shorthand with the assumption that Carolyn understood what I was thinking. It's the sort of thing a retailer might do when assuming a customer knows why a price on a favorite item has increased or the delivery of a special order has been delayed. It's the sort of thing that can lead to misunderstandings of motivations.

In the following chapters, my objective is to dissolve any misunderstandings, retailer, about the primary motivators for giving both you and your shoppers what it takes to achieve a sense of well-being. Calling on my experience in researching, consulting, and training with my RIMtailing services, I'll address the subtleties, caution you against impressions which might mean the opposite of what's commonly assumed, and suggest techniques for using the information to improve your profitability.

Let's sell well-being and sell it well. As retail professionals, let us transform the epigram "Money can't buy happiness" into the motto "Whoever said money can't buy happiness just didn't know where to shop."

Then let's motivate people not only to shop with us, but also to go on to buy from us.

Oh, one more thing: At my seafood dinner in Modesto, California that night, Carolyn came back after a few minutes and, without saying a word, curtly dropped one additional cloth napkin onto the table.

RIMinders

- Stay vigilant to the dangers in assuming your intended customers make purchase decisions in the same ways you do. Similarly, be aware that what you intend to say to a shopper may not be what the shopper thinks you intend. Be ready to clarify by giving further information.
- Emphasize possibilities, not statistical probabilities, to shoppers.
- Accommodate the cycles in your customers' purchasing behavior.
- Give customers the tools to look at what they have on their shelves and in the cabinets at home before coming to your store.
- To avoid misunderstandings, use "not" and "no" only selectively in your communications with consumers.
- Demonstrate to your shoppers that money can buy happiness, whether that happiness arises from excitement or serenity.

2

Value

~⌇

Why would somebody pay £78,000—the equivalent of about $126,000 in the U.S. at the time—for a dress designed by a woman whose name was relatively unknown inside or outside fashion circles? The answer is that the dress had been worn by someone whose name, Kate Middleton, promptly garnered celebrity-quality recognition when it was revealed she'd be marrying Prince William in Westminster Abbey.

The phenomenon is nothing new. In year 2004, an eBay buyer dropped more than $15,000 for a gob of gum chewed by Brittany Spears. Somebody paid $48,875 for Jackie Kennedy's tape measure. Convicted swindler Bernie Madoff's blue Mets jacket, looking very much the same as many other blue Mets jackets, sold for $14,500.

Researchers at Yale University and Israel's Bar-Ilan University[12] explored the shopper psychology behind the phenomenon. They asked study participants how much they'd like to own specified common artifacts such as clothing and furniture which had previously been used by celebrities or non-celebrities. Some of the celebrity names were well-regarded. George Clooney, for instance. Others had a markedly less positive reputation. Saddam Hussein, for example.

As expected, the participants assigned higher value to celebrity-associated items. When the association was with a well-regarded name, the consumers' explanation was prestige by physical association. The consumers felt they could actually absorb some of the remnants of the original owner. Consistent with this, those study participants said that if the item had been thoroughly cleaned, it was nowhere near as valuable to them. However, if purchase of the item included a requirement it could not be resold, this didn't decrease the attractiveness much at all.

With the negatively regarded celebrities, like Messrs. Madoff and Hussein, the effect was reversed. Sterilization of the item before purchase was all to the good. But prohibitions on resale dramatically decreased the valuation by the consumers in the study. Here the purchase was being made as an investment.

A sense of value motivates consumers, but the process of valuing is more complex than many retailers assume. A phenomenon called "contagious magic" by consumer psychologists is one of the many subtleties playing into valuing.

"Please use this high-end putter to attempt ten shots on this artificial green. Here's the putter," said the research scientists at Max Planck Institute for Biological Cybernetics[13] to each of a group of right-handed golfers. For half the number of study participants, selected at random, when each was handed the putter, he or she was also told something like, "This putter I'm handing you was used in the past by Professional Golfers' Association player Ben Curtis." Mr. Curtis had won the PGA Tour four times. His total career winnings exceeded $13 million.

Compared to the study participants not given the additional announcement, those who were led to believe they were using the golf club previously held by Mr. Curtis sank a third more of the putts into the hole on average. There's also reason to believe they found the task easier: When all the study participants were asked to draw a picture of the hole before attempting the shots, Curtis-primed golfers produced drawings 9% larger.

Contagious magic refers to the belief—commonly encountered in consumers and usually subconscious—that two objects which touch will exert an influence on each other. That's what was going on in this study, with the contagious magic endowing confidence.

A study at Arizona State University and New Zealand's University of Auckland[14] used musicians in place of duffers, guitars in place of putters, and supposed replicas in place of supposed actual possessions. Why is it, the researchers asked, that a purchaser of a guitar would find that having a respected rock star sign the guitar caused the guitar to produce better music? This was especially true when the guitar was a replica of the instrument used by the rock star autographing it. The answer: Contagious magic!

Merchandise in your store which carries a logo or label associated with prestige—such as Lacoste—can command premium prices because shoppers assume they'll receive greater respect when others observe the logo. These shopper are accurate, at least to a point. Researchers at Tilburg University[15] found that a man shown wearing a Lacoste or Tommy Hilfiger polo shirt was judged by study participants to be of higher status and wealthier than the same man wearing a no-label shirt, although the label didn't make a difference on ratings for kindness, trustworthiness, or attractiveness.

However, you might decide to stock items where the logo is not obviously displayed. There are consumers who prefer a secret handshake. Researchers at University of Pennsylvania and Southern Methodist University[16] note how consumers of very high-end products often prefer subtle, not obvious, signals in their purchases. Consider sunglasses. The researcher's tally found that about 20% of sunglasses selling for under $50 included a brand name or logo easily visible to others. That increased to about 85% when the retail price was between $100 and $300, but for sunglasses selling above the $500 mark, the percentage dropped dramatically. It was only about 30%.

Consumers who sense themselves coming closer to desired membership in a group, but who are insecure about their membership, tend to purchase products that loudly project the signals of membership. But when the consumer already belongs to an exclusive group or is confidently aspiring to belong, they'll be looking for more subtle cues—what corresponds to the secret handshake which allows members to recognize each other while not tipping off the outsiders. This was another lesson learned by Lacoste, which discovered that their crocodile logo stopped portraying as much status if it was displayed too prominently.

A distinctive shopping bag your customers display to others can gain you customers. It's like the effect of people seeing customers using what they purchased at your store.

Researchers at Northwestern University and University of Pennsylvania[17] applied this principle to the purchase of new cars because the consumer had seen others driving that make and model. The effect was larger among commuters than non-commuters, probably because commuters have more opportunities to observe the relative frequency with which people have selected various automobiles.

With shopping bags, the effect is likely to be larger if your store is in a mall rather than isolated. Still, if the shopping bag is sturdy enough for reuse, it should get more exposure and thus influence more prospects.

The effect is stronger on people similar to the purchaser. In the car study, seeing vehicles associated with male traits of power and flash had greater influence on purchases by men than by women. Similarly, preferences were changed only among cars in a parallel price tier. The Toyota Corolla prospect was not greatly influenced by seeing lots of people driving Lexus models. With shopping bags, a budget logo will influence budget shoppers more than luxury shoppers.

Think what tag line you'd like to put on the bag along with your logo so it draws notice from your target psychological profiles.

Other research suggests the shopping bag's effectiveness derives from the mindset of the customer carrying the bag and how that mindset is observed by passersby. University of Minnesota[18] researchers had female participants lug around a shopping bag for an hour as they walked through a mall. Some of the women carried a Victoria's Secret shopping bag. The rest carried a pink shopping bag with no store or brand identification. At the end of the hour, each woman returned to the research site and was asked to rate herself on a list of personality traits.

Compared to those who carried the plain bag, the women who carried the Victoria's Secret bag were more likely to rate themselves as feminine, glamorous, and physically attractive. These are characteristics associated with the Victoria's Secret store and merchandise brands. The packaging in which an item is carried influences the value the consumer places on the item.

The shape of the package on the shelf also makes a difference. When shoppers are presented with two unfamiliar products in a category—one of the products in an unusually-shaped container and the other one not—most shoppers believe they're getting more for their money with the product in the unusual container. The unusual shape draws more attention, and the consumer's brain subconsciously translates the extra attention into higher value.

Valuation is affected by the package and also by the package deal. As we saw in the last chapter, attraction to package deals varies with time since paycheck. Valuation of the package deal is also, as you'd expect, affected by what's combined into the deal. But perhaps not in a way you'd expect.

A consumer electronics store charges $2,000 for a high-definition television and $10 for a video cable. How much would consumers be willing to pay for the two items together? Maybe $2,005, with the customer figuring that the retailer has already made enough profit on the HDTV sale?

How about $1,950? Less than the price of the HDTV on its own. That's what researchers at Pepperdine University and Northwestern University[19] discovered. Participants in their study said they'd pay $2,000 for the television and they'd pay $10 for the cable, but later said they'd expect to pay $1,950 for the combination.

The reason seems to be that grafting an inexpensive item onto an expensive item cheapens the price image of the expensive item. The same phenomenon occurred when the researchers paired a tote bag with a premium-priced suitcase. It happens with other product categories like scooters, barbeque grills, telephones, jackets, and backpacks. On average, consumers' acceptable price points decreased by about 25% when a trinket was added onto a treasure. Of equal concern is that consumer interest in purchasing the expensive item decreased by about 15%.

One remedy is to wait until the shopper has made the decision to purchase the expensive item and then offer the inexpensive item as a thank-you gift. You might earn gratitude from the surprise, even though the item is viewed as a trinket.

A better way to avoid the price depreciation is to point out the synergy in the two or more items you're offering. Talk about how the items bring out the best in each other. This dissolves the shopper's impression that the inexpensive item has been grafted onto the expensive one. This impression is, after all, what's behind the decrease in willingness to pay.

Describe to the potential purchaser how well the various functions work together. Instead of focusing on the different capabilities, focus on the added benefits that come from the combination.

So including more items in a package deal often adds to the shopper's valuation of the package, but not always. In the same vein, featuring more benefits of an item usually adds to its valuation, but not always. This twist has to do with pleasure versus practicality.

Consumers make decisions for a mix of practical, utilitarian reasons and pleasure-seeking, hedonic reasons. The utilitarian is to get a job done. The hedonic is to indulge oneself. When buying a power saw, the utilitarian is to have a way to cut things and the hedonic is to experience pride in the clean cuts. Even though there's always a mix of the two, either the utilitarian or the hedonic often predominates. With the power saw, the utilitarian is probably more important to the shopper. With a ticket to a concert, it's probably the hedonic.

As consumers mature from childhood, they place progressively less importance on the sheer number of attributes of an item being considered for purchase. With adult consumers, the number of attributes is more important when it comes to hedonic than utilitarian products and services.

One explanation for the greater importance of a tally of features when it comes to hedonic items is that consumers feel a need for more justification to make the purchase. Another explanation is that people are more interested in a variety of experiences with hedonic items. Even if we love thinking about the chocolate in what we're eating, occasionally switching to thoughts about the accompanying raisins makes it more fun.

With child consumers, the more attributes of benefit to the shopper, the better. With adults, pack in the attribute claims for hedonic items. For items which the adult shopper might buy primarily for utilitarian reasons, keep up the value estimate by pruning down the attribute list.

Researchers at New York University and University of Florida[20] looked at what happens with ads designed to promote consumption of an entire product category. Examples included the Florida Citrus Board's ads for orange juice and the Midwest Dairy Association's "Ah, the power of cheese" campaign. Such advertising intends to increase overall demand, but not selectively favor certain members of the advertising group funding the ads.

The researchers discovered that the outcomes frequently fell far short of this objective. I'm a great fan of merchants collaborating with each other as a retailing community. However, be careful with trade association advertising. When the generic ads for orange juice emphasized nutritional advantages, this helped the Albertsons store brand more than it did the premium Tropicana brand. The effect was the other way around when the generic ads emphasized the value of good flavor.

We might assume that the value of a featured advantage—such as nutrition or flavor—will grow in the consumer's mind, while the importance of the other advantages will not be disturbed. Talking about nutrition doesn't decrease the value of flavor for the consumer, it's said. But the research disproved the assumption. With utilitarian items, an ad highlighting nutrition will lead to the consumer placing less value on other attributes, such as flavor.

What's hedonic and what's utilitarian, as well as which attributes and benefits stand out, depend on the shopper's objectives. Therefore, when you ask a shopper for their objective in making the purchase, use the answer to figure out which product attributes are of primary importance.

In a study by researchers at University of Missouri, Mississippi State University, Emory University, and University of California-Irvine,[21] most participants said that a granola bar was more like a candy bar than like a cup of fruit yogurt. But for the people who placed high priority on good health, the granola bar was more like a cup of fruit yogurt. Those same health-oriented consumers said an apple was more like an orange than like a donut. But for the people who placed a higher priority on eating convenience than on eating healthy, the apple-donut similarity came up stronger.

The category in which a shopper places a product determines the comparisons they'll make in deciding what to buy from you. If you're selling apples, donuts, and oranges, the health-oriented customers will be comparing the prices, the freshness, and other attributes of the apples with the oranges. The convenience-first customers will be doing an apple-donut comparison.

If you're selling flowerpots, statuary, and seed flats, the dedicated gardener looks for the flowerpots and seed flats to be in the same shopping area. The dedicated outdoor decorator wants to compare the aesthetic attributes of the flowerpots with the statuary.

We can guide the choices of our shoppers by the ways in which we arrange the merchandise and by how we describe the alternatives we give the shoppers for spending their money. But it often works better to present the alternatives in terms of what categories we discover our shoppers already using.

What if the products being considered have similar valued attributes? When two options have some features in common, the shopper tends to ignore those features and place extra attention on valued attributes distinctive in each option. This selective attention carries over to additional choices shown afterwards to the shopper. Therefore, as a retailer, you can influence which valued attributes the shopper will emphasize in considerations: Start by showing two choice alternatives which share the valued attributes you prefer the shopper not emphasize.

A shopper's objectives also determine attributes they dislike. Research at University of Memphis and Indiana University[22] assessed the situation where consumers are comparing two products which both have unwanted attributes, but each of the two has distinctive positive attributes. Again, the distinctive attributes get an emphasis. The consumer becomes less likely to consider the negative attributes in deciding among the alternatives. Here, also, this effect established with the comparison of two carries over to immediately subsequent comparisons.

Moreover, people carry into your store with them one or another preconception about characteristics of products. Researchers at Babson College[23] asked shoppers at a Boston-area liquor store to sip a wine, then give their judgment of the quality. Some of the study participants were told the wine was from Italy, while others were told the wine was from India. The wine samples were from the same lot.

The timing of the country-of-origin statement determined how the stereotype operated, and in that fact resides the advice for retailers: If the wine-taster was given the country-of-origin information before the sip, those tasting the "Italian" wine rated the product as having higher quality than did those tasting the wine from "India." If the information was given after the sip, the results were reversed: Those who had sipped the "Italian" wine gave lower ratings to the quality on average than those getting the wine from the same bottle, but told it was from India.

It was as if the consumer who had enjoyed the experience went overboard in fighting against the common stereotype that Italian wines are better than Indian wines. The researchers found parallel results with studies involving chocolates being identified as coming from either Switzerland or China, playing on the stereotype of Swiss chocolate being superior.

When country-of-origin information helps you make the sale, feature it. Featuring it means presenting country-of-origin information well before you present other information about the product. Talk about it in ads a shopper would see before arranging to come to buy from you. To feature country-of-origin information in personal selling, state it as the first item and pause for a few seconds after saying it so the information starts brewing in the shopper's brain.

If country-of-origin information elicits an immediate negative reaction in a consumer, the emotion can be eased by asking the consumer to visualize positive scenes involving the country or by surrounding the shopper in-store with pleasant memorabilia from the country. You might also choose to downplay the country of origin.

Corona beer successfully accomplished this. As Corona climbed to its position as the second most popular imported beer, it was nicknamed "Mexican lemonade," and rumors circulated that workers urinated into the beer during the manufacturing process. Retailers began pulling the beer from shelves. In response, the U.S. Corona distributor filed a lawsuit against a Reno, Nevada Heineken beer distributor for originating the rumor. But more important, Corona provided retailers with the tools to position the beverage not so much as a Mexican beer as a beer of the beach. It worked.

The counterpoint of adding value with foreign-country-of-origin claims is touting "Buy Local." Does the shopper's mind operate differently if the manufacturing location is presented as a local county rather than a distant country?

Researchers at Drexel University and Concordia University[24] say it does in at least one way: The consumer assessing a locally produced item will place an especially high importance on accurately assessing the quality of the item. Quality is less likely to be questioned when the item has the recognized national pedigree. Valuing the local is most powerful when the retailer has worked to convince the shopper there's no reason to doubt item quality.

There's more than quality, though. Consumers can be motivated to buy local because of their local loyalties, or stop buying if the neighborhood touch gets lost. Back to the beer: When InBev bought St. Louis-based Anheuser-Busch to form the world's largest brewing company, with operations in over 30 countries and sales in over 130 countries and then fired 1,000 St. Louis area employees, the St. Louis populace found it tougher to view Bud as a local brand made good. Over the next two years, the number of taps serving Schlafly Beer, brewed only in St. Louis, climbed more than 30%. The solitary concession stand selling Schlafly at Busch Stadium was joined by seven others.

Another implication of "place" in shopper's valuation has to do with convenience. The general rule is to make it as easy as possible for shoppers to locate and use any merchandise we want to sell them. But as with all other good rules, there are exceptions. When the shopper has searched long and hard for an item, finally finding it in your store, the item can command a premium price. Difficulty bestows value.

Consider results from a classic study at University of Texas-Arlington.[25] Researchers investigated the relationship between the taste of a potato chip and the ease of opening the package. For some participants, the potato chips were packaged in a wax-coated bag which could be easily opened. For the other participants, the polyvinyl bag was so difficult to open that participants resorted to techniques like using their teeth or standing on the bag while pulling at a seam.

In blind tests conducted before the main study, whether the chips were in the wax-coated bag or the polyvinyl bag had no effect on people's ratings of crispness or overall taste—as long as the researcher, not the participant, opened the package and served the chips. But when the participants had to open their own packages, which of the two types of bag resulted in higher ratings of crispness and taste?

Yes, the polyvinyl bag.

Asking people, "Which tastes better?," is not the same as asking, "Which would you probably buy?" People often settle for a lower quality alternative when they can get to it more easily or inexpensively. If deciding between providing your product in the equivalent of the wax-coated bag or the polyvinyl bag, you might choose the less burdensome alternative. But if your product comes with necessary barriers to usage, look for ways to leverage those negatives so as to increase the perceived value of the item.

Consumers overall want ease of use and turnkey solutions. Still, consumers who are interested in being productive in their lives value collecting the experiences a challenge provides.

A challenge is especially likely to increase valuation, and therefore persuasion, in consumers who consider themselves ready to meet the challenge. It's true in the collection of donations. University of Chicago[26] researchers found that people who described themselves as "pioneers" dropped higher amounts of money into a charity box when they had to stretch four feet to make the contribution rather than just drop it in without stretching. This difference did not appear among people describing themselves as "followers."

It's true with interpersonal choices. Heterosexual men were shown photos of potential female dates and asked to judge each woman's attractiveness. Some of the photos were crystal clear, while the other photos were out of focus by 15%. Those men who had described themselves as "smooth talkers" found the women in the blurry photos to be more attractive than those in the crystal clear photos. Meeting the challenge of decoding the blurry photo added to the attractiveness. On the other hand, the men describing themselves as "shy gawkers" judged the women in the clear photos as better looking.

Of most relevance to you, it's true in retail stores. Shoppers who characterized themselves as "smart" rather than "not smart" expressed a higher preference for products they'd have to travel across town to get over equivalent products they could purchase nearby. These shoppers also evaluated products more positively if the products had been pushed back on the shelves rather than being in easy reach.

When George Herbert Leigh Mallory was asked why he wanted to climb Mount Everest, his reputed response became what has been termed the most famous three words in mountaineering: "Because it's there." The need to overcome barriers can make the objective more valuable to the consumer.

RIMinders

- To increase the apparent value of an item, associate its use with a celebrity.
- Build identification with your store by having people wear or carry an item bearing your store logo.
- For very high-end shoppers, display luxury logos in a subtle format.
- To increase apparent value, display the items in a way that stands out from the surroundings.
- Avoid offering package deals which combine an expensive with an unrelated inexpensive item.
- With primarily pleasure-oriented items, describe enough item attributes to allow the shopper to justify the purchase. With primarily utilitarian items, like toilet tissue, there are fewer selling advantages from a long attribute list, and a longer list of purchase benefits will dilute the impact of each benefits claim.
- To have the shopper place higher value on an item characteristic important to that shopper, show comparison alternatives that have other desirable attributes, but not the one you want the shopper to highlight.
- When country-of-origin information helps you make the sale, present country-of-origin information well before you present other information about the product.
- To encourage "Buy Local," place high importance on the benefits to the local community, but even higher importance on the quality of the items.
- Stay alert to circumstances in which increasing the difficulty of consumption would increase the value of the item for the purchaser.

3

Values

~⁙

Ever notice how when the items in your store are in short supply, your male shoppers with a last name like Wallace are likely to place their orders sooner than male shoppers with a last name like Baker?

Probably not, since you're too busy to be paying attention to what seems like such a strange influence on purchase behavior. But researchers at Georgetown University and Belmont University[27] had a hunch from prior research that there was what they coined a "last name effect," and they did pay attention.

Boys whose last names come later in the alphabet become accustomed to having to wait longer. In the classroom, they're more likely to sit in the back of the room, and on the playground, they're more likely to be placed later in the line. So when they grow up into adult male consumers, they're concerned only the scraps will be left for them unless they act fast.

The researchers verified the last name effect with opportunities to choose a bottle of wine, take advantage of a limited-time discount on a backpack, get four free tickets to attend a top-ranked women's basketball game, and enter a drawing for a $500 prize. The effect was weaker for women than for men. That's to be expected since it depends on childhood experiences, and married women often use their husband's surname.

This last name effect influences how quickly consumers respond to direct mail offers, replace items such as roofs and cars, and learn to use the latest technologies. In each of these, any marketing appeal which emphasizes getting a head start will pack an extra punch with the men and never-married women on your mailing list whose surnames begin late in the alphabet.

Childhood experiences do influence consumer behavior, including values.

"I'm a Yankees fan," announces the New York City school teacher to her class. "Who else in our classroom roots for the Yankees to always win?"

All the students enthusiastically raise their hands. Except for Erica.

Puzzled, the teacher asks, "Erica, why aren't you raising your hand?"

I'm not a Yankees fan, Miss Fredericks. I root for the Boston Red Sox."

Now even more puzzled, Miss Fredericks asks Erica, "How could you possibly be a Red Sox fan?"

"Because my mom and my dad are both Red Sox fans."

Sensing a teachable moment for the class, Ms. Fredericks moves into lecture mode. "You know, you don't always have to be exactly like your parents. You can be your own person and still love them." Then, gaining momentum, the teacher goes on. "Erica, what if your mom and your dad were absolute morons. What do you think you'd be then?"

"Well, probably a Yankees fan."

Children and adults alike select products, services, activities, and ideas with attention to family loyalty and family pride. There's an even greater pull when the family itself or the object of choice is an underdog.

People like to help out a friend, particularly if the friend is at a disadvantage. This drive carries over to their relationships with stores and brands. Researchers at Harvard University, Simmons College, and Boston College[28] found that when a choice of chocolate bar brands was offered to study participants, the brand positioned as the underdog was selected about 70% of the time.

Caring about the underdog—the less able—is a universal part of human beings' values systems. Visitors to our stores show a special attraction to products and services for their children, and when they don't have children, to their pets.

There's indeed gold from them thar dogs. And cats. And rabbits, reptiles, birds, gerbils, fish, and more. The profitability enjoyed by retailers offering items for pets often verifies an Eastern Washington University[29] research finding: People are more willing to buy premium items for their pets than for themselves. About 80% of dog owners said they were serious about selecting healthy food for their dogs, but only 65% of the same people said they were serious about their own food selection.

People generally consider their pets to be defenseless. It's the same dynamic that helps explain why, during economic downturns, most consumers cut back more on expenses for themselves than on expenses for their offspring.

Adults might not have as much splurge-spirit love for Henrietta the hamster as for Hank the family dog. But compared to owners of a cat or a dog, adults having fish or reptiles are more likely to also have kids around. Nearly 90% of households with a hamster include children. And for those children, there's no question that Henrietta is worth a splurge. Just be sure you merchandise those indulgent items for pets at the children's eye level.

At the same time, there's a growth in households without children. As this percentage of families with children decreases, the drive to own a pet increases. Some of the decrease comes from people staying single longer, some comes from empty nesters living longer, and some from other sources. Researchers at *American Demographic* reported that 92% of owners of dogs and cats consider the animals to be members of the family, and about 75% of household cats and dogs receive gifts on holidays and their birthdays.

Whatever your retailing line, it would benefit you to carry products of special interest to pet owners. Almost any retailer can include at least a limited line. Harley-Davidson, Ralph Lauren, IKEA, and Lands' End have all done it. Services retailers, too, would benefit by thinking about ways to sell to pet-owner markets. People board their birds as well as their dogs.

And if it won't work for you to allow the pet to join the shoppers in your store, develop a warm spot in your shoppers' hearts by featuring photos of pets with their people.

Do be aware of limits on how cute your regular customers will let you get. There are those likely to consider your store to be foolish for catering at all to health-oriented pet items. Dog owners are more nurturing of their pets than cat owners are of theirs. The psychology of the cat owner, along with the feline itself, is one of greater independence. And an aquarium owner I know about commented sarcastically on the health trend, "I feed my goldfish organic, wild caught (not farmed) fish food. I am hoping they live 7 months instead of 6."

If rather than pets or children, the basis of a purchase decision is allegiance to the customer's country, we could call it patriotism, and this imparts an extra angle to the country-of-origin influences I discussed in the last chapter. With families, there are also the genes. Researchers at Stanford University and University of Florida-Gainesville[30] identified likings for specific products having a genetic component, such that if one member of the family likes it, there's a good chance others in the family will, too. This can be helpful to you in making sales when a family is shopping together at your store and in guiding gift selections. The eclectic list of product categories includes chocolate, mustard, hybrid cars, science fiction movies, and jazz.

Political affiliation influences purchasing behavior for reasons of both genetics and family environment. If many of your shoppers identify themselves as religious and say they vote Republican, emphasize national brands over store brands in your merchandising and hesitate stocking just-released products. However, once you've established the habit of coming to your store among these consumers, you can stray from the merchandising formula without destroying the habit.

This advice follows from findings at University of Michigan, New York University, and Turkey's Özyeğin University.[31] The researchers analyzed actual purchases over a six-year period in 1,860 supermarkets across 416 U.S. counties. Survey data on voting patterns and religiosity for each county were used to calculate what the researchers identified as "conservatism."

The conservatives' significant preference for national brands and aversion to newly-released products was seen across almost all of the 26 product categories evaluated. The researchers caution that all the product categories they assessed were utilitarian (diapers, peanut butter, and toothpaste, for instance) rather than hedonic (fashions, candy, wine, or bath oils, for example). But my store experience indicates the conservative's attraction to tradition carries over to hedonic items.

Republicans prefer to have decision making decentralized. They think of political leaders as reliable and practical, but as not paying enough attention to what's best for the locals. Democrats see politicians as intelligent, empathic, and interested in individual needs, so the Democrats are more willing to grant centralized authority. The Republicans favor stores like Subway, where you make a series of discrete choices yourself. Democrats tend to go down the street to Wendy's, where you're encouraged to order by prepaid package number.

Republicans, more than Democrats, fear for the future of free enterprise. In surveys, they, on average, preferred Allstate, which had mounted fear-based ad campaigns, to Progressive, which featured smiling reassurance. Democrats preferred Progressive to Allstate. They fear we're losing a healthy environment. For them, Jeep trumps BMW, and Starbucks beats out Dunkin' Donuts. Republicans see it the other way around, in general.

Salespeople in small to midsize retail businesses can get to know their customers well, and in doing so, distinguish among values systems which would strike others as virtually identical. Such as distinguishing cheapskates from frugal shoppers.

Cheapskates—also known as tightwads—are an underappreciated market. When you survey tightwads, they admit to making smaller purchases than they think they should. Tightwads believe they should be willing to spend more money. And tightwads have the money to spend. Annual income is similar for tightwads compared to spendthrifts, who believe they should be spending less. Tightwads don't feel poor, and their shopping behavior isn't driven as in those who fret about the future because of worldwide economic difficulties. Tightwads aren't the same as frugal shoppers. Frugality is driven by a pleasure in saving. Tightwads are driven by a pain of paying.

Women are no more likely to be tightwads than spendthrifts. However, men are three times more likely to be tightwads than spendthrifts. Consumers under the age of 30 are only slightly more likely to be tightwads than spendthrifts, but respondents over 70 are five times more likely to be tightwads than spendthrifts.

The key to having tightwads spend their money with you is to reinforce their sense of responsibility.

- Congratulate tightwads on how they shop carefully. Tightwads take pride in limiting their spending, but feel more comfortable when loosening up within reason.
- Remind tightwads that you'll be responsible in what you sell to them. Then keep your promise by explaining how the products and services you offer give full value. Remember that tightwads suffer emotional pain when spending. Dealing with a responsible retailer eases the pain.
- Accentuate the small. Based on a survey administered to more than 13,000 adults, researchers at University of Pennsylvania and Carnegie Mellon University[32] identified a group of consumers who said they hated spending money on items beyond necessities. These people met the definition of tightwad. In the next stage of the study, the tightwads were offered the opportunity to pay extra for overnight shipping of a DVD they wanted. The extra cost was presented to some tightwads as "a $5 fee" and to the rest of the tightwads as "a small $5 fee." The tightwads hearing the word "small" were 20% more likely to pay the fee than those not hearing that word. In contrast, there was no difference with a "$5" and "small $5" description among people who were spendthrifts—people who indicated on the earlier survey the opposite of tightwad tendencies.
- Don't tell tightwads about opportunity costs. In advertising and selling, opportunity cost appeals take the form, "By paying less for this item, you'll have more money available to buy other items." Spendthrifts respond to opportunity cost appeals, but tightwads are much less responsive. This is because tightwads have already figured out the opportunity-cost angles for themselves. They'd consider a retailer telling them about opportunity costs to be a waste of time, and tightwads hate to waste.

Values change over the life span. That fact was behind an impressive cross-selling success. In cross-selling, we aim to sell to the purchaser additional related products and services. Suppose there were a way to increase your cross-selling success by 56% in the short-term. Researchers at Indiana University and Carnegie Mellon University[33] say they've found such a way.

That's the short-term. You're in retailing for the long-term. The researchers report even more compelling statistics here, saying they were able to increase the long-term response rate to cross-selling marketing by about 150%, resulting in an increase of almost 180% in long-term profit.

The setting was a financial institution. The cross-selling consisted of educating the customer about other financial products which could benefit them. What made the difference, the researchers say, was the timing of the education. People go through life changes in rather predictable patterns. With financial services, the researchers found that consumers begin their relationship with a firm by seeking convenience, then move toward wanting flexibility in money management, and then toward stimulation from investment risk. When the nature of the education was timed to fit life changes, cross-selling was dramatically more successful.

When your customers feel they've been able to express their values while choosing an item to purchase, they'll enjoy the product more. They'll also enjoy the shopping experience more. The motivation to return to your store soon and often will blossom.

The other side of this is that you shouldn't expect customers to express as much enjoyment of products they've selected from habit, and they're less likely to brag about what transpired when they shopped at your store for those choices. To increase the consumer's enjoyment of these purchases and the accompanying purchase experiences, look for opportunities to make it a choice.

In many cases, you won't be able to do this, since the shopper wants to finish as quickly as possible. In other cases, though, you can discuss with the customer the product attributes important to them in that product category and then describe how a few of the items weigh in on those attributes.

Researchers at University of Chicago and Korea University[34] had consumers make selections in seven product categories—coffee blends, novels, music CDs, video games, magazines, DVD titles, and calendar designs. Some of the study participants were asked to choose from each category the one item which best expressed their tastes and values. The other study participants were asked to choose for each category one alternative to satisfy a need to have an item in that category. As each participant went through the succession of seven choices, they were periodically asked to report how tired or energized they felt and how interested they were in the product they selected.

The researchers found that as participants went through the series of choices, the "express your values" ones reported becoming more energized, while those in the "satisfy a need" group reported becoming more tired. In addition, the people in the first group reported higher interest in choices than did those in the second group.

These results are what you might expect as an experienced retailer, but one of the implications might have missed your attention: By decreasing a shopper's driving need to buy a product in a certain category, you'll increase interest in the product.

These influences of values on shopping choices are tendencies, not certainties, and often operate below the level of conscious awareness. In fact, consumers usually find it emotionally challenging to consciously consider the whole truth. One realm in which this challenge has been seen is the shopper's sense of social responsibility.

Your customer loves the design of a shirt on your store shelf, but despises the labor practices of manufacturers of certain products your store carries. So the customer doesn't look at the label before putting the shirt into their shopping cart.

Your customer instantly realizes the mahogany table now on your showroom floor would look perfect in their dining room, but they could never look themselves in the eye if they thought the mahogany came from an endangered rain forest. So they don't give it a thought.

This willful ignorance operates subconsciously, and it occurs because handling the full truth would be overly painful for the person.

Shoppers who care the most about an issue are the ones most likely to hide from the reality. The furniture shopper who would feel the deepest amount of grief at having in their home any wood from an endangered rainforest turns out to be the shopper most likely to avoid asking about the origin of the material after they've decided they deeply love the item for sale.

Willful ignorance happens when strong emotions—like grief and love—are in conflict. This occurs not only with matters of social consciousness, but also with issues like price, delivery time, and installation difficulty. In relationships with merchandise as with humans, once love sets it, we subconsciously avoid asking too many questions that could lead to values conflicts.

Decide how much information you and your sales staff should volunteer. As a rule, I'm against overloading customers with information or answering questions that haven't be asked. However, the nature of willful ignorance is such that doubts are quite likely to bubble to the surface after the purchase. This can lead your customer to be sorry they made the purchase from you and even to blame you for withholding information from them.

If you sense something is important for the customer to know, tell it to them. When withheld information leads to values conflicts, product characteristics can be misperceived.

Researchers at Southern Methodist University and University of Texas-Austin[35] watched what happened when people from UT were assigned to purchase a present for someone who wanted an item carrying the logo of UT archrival Texas A&M. The reactions were compared to those of a comparable group assigned to buy a gift emblazoned with the UT Longhorns logo.

The researchers report that when selecting the item for the Texas A&M fan, the shoppers fidgeted, chewed on their lips, and averted their eyes. They crossed their arms, as if to distance themselves from what they were doing, and at the cash/wrap, they actually stepped away from the item, as if to say to anybody watching, "Don't think this item represents who I really am."

Then the researchers provided relief. They offered to each participant a choice between an expensive silver pen with no logo or a low-priced plastic pen with the Longhorn logo. Those who had bought the Texas A&M gift were more likely to select the cheap pen.

The lesson for you, retailer? Carry items that allow customers to affirm their desired identities. Then get the shopper to sign off on it.

While I was shopping for a new Toyota years ago, a salesman asked me to sign my name on a blank index card. I'd made what I considered to be my final price offer. He said, "To show that you're serious, I'll ask you to put your signature on this index card. I'll take it along with your offer to the sales manager."

As a set of University of Alberta[36] researchers point out, the act of writing our signature has more than legal implications. The act is tied to our psychological identity.

In one study, the researchers selected a group of consumers who considered running as a sport to be an important part of their self-image and another group who did not. Some of the people in each of the two groups were asked to print their names as part of a task, while the rest of the people were asked to write their signature. Then each of the study participants was asked to shop for a pair of running shoes while the researchers watched.

Among those people who considered running an important component of their self-identity, those who had written their signature ended up spending more time in the store and trying on more running shoes than those who had been asked to print their name.

Wait a second! Was spending more time in the store trying on more shoes a good outcome? Wouldn't we prefer to have customers come in, make a purchase quickly, and leave? No, not really. Those who spend more time in the store are likely to see more items to buy. The research findings indicated that signing the name accomplished this by strengthening an association between the customer's self-identity and the personality of the store. So we'd expect to see more repeat business.

All this was not true, however, for the study participants who did not associate their identity with running as a sport. In fact, those who had signed their names spent less time in the store than those who had printed their names.

That car salesman's execution of the tactic with me was flawed. I refused to sign a blank index card. Still, the tactic itself has research support: If a customer identifies with your store or a product there, having them sign their name—such as to register for a prize drawing—usually strengthens the store-customer or product-customer identification.

In another University of Texas-Austin study, this one in partnership with Switzerland's University of Bern,[37] researchers looked at the emotional attachment of a total of more than 2,300 consumers to a total of 167 brands retailers carry. They found that consumers are more likely to form an emotional attachment to an item at retail if the consumer sees the item as fitting their image of their current self rather than of the person they aspire to be. Shoppers hesitate reaching out too far.

But maintaining the status quo will result in smaller shopping basket totals. We'd prefer our shoppers to find happiness via aspiring to more. To trigger aspiration, build the shopper's self-esteem. One technique for doing this is to flatter the shopper's expertise. A motivator for many experts is showing off their knowledge.

For the best long-term results, give genuine praise. However, even insincere flattery can be effective, according to researchers at Hong Kong University of Science and Technology.[38]

In their set of studies, prospective clothing shoppers were given a flyer advertising a department store. The flyer read, "We're contacting you because you're fashionable and stylish," and then asked the shopper to visit the store.

It seemed to me that such obviously insincere flattery would at best amuse a shopper and at worst annoy them. I was surprised to learn that, due to the flattery, shoppers rated the store more highly. Still, not all the shoppers did. More about that in a minute.

In a second experiment, participants were offered a discount coupon from the store that gave the flattery or from a store whose flyer offered no flattery. About 80% of shoppers chose the coupon from the phony-flattery store. But only under certain conditions.

In the third experiment, flattered participants were told that the store charged especially high prices and had a restricted range of clothing. Even when confronted with these negatives, participants held onto their positive views. Unless those consumers agreed to do a certain thing first.

Since I hope you'll apply these insights to your retailing, I'll tell you the rest of the story:

In the first experiment, the phony flattery had the clearest effect when participants were told they had only five seconds to respond to each question about how much they liked the store.

In the second experiment, the 80% figure was from shoppers who chose the coupon three days after reading the phony flattery. For those who chose the coupon right after reading it, the figure was substantially less, at 54%.

In the third experiment, the negative information did push the ratings toward the negative if the participants, before receiving the phony flattery, were made to feel good about themselves by agreeing to write down a positive trait they believed themselves to have.

When dealing with customers hungry for self-esteem, phony flattery can facilitate sales. This works best if the customer is distracted from thinking about the flattery having been phony, such as by being rushed or making a selection after some time has passed.

As I'll aim to show in Chapter 9, each time you personalize the selling message to a characteristic of the shopper, you're building the shopper's self-esteem. Even the smallest things can give you a retailer's edge. Researchers at Universiteit Leuven in Belgium[39] found that across languages and cultures, people's self-esteem is heightened a bit not only when their name is used, but also when they are shown or given products with brand names starting with the first letter in their own names.

In a report of results I consider to be even stranger, Clark University researchers in collaboration with colleagues at Babson College[40] say that when an item's price resembles the sound of the shopper's name or birthdate, the shopper will like the price better. In some circumstances, this means the shopper will prefer that price to a lower price which sounds nothing like the shopper's identifying information. A price of fifty-five dollars has extra appeal for consumers named Fred or Ms. Fine. A price of $49.15 has extra appeal for a consumer born on 9/15 or even 4/15.

You may not set different prices for different shoppers based on an individual's name or birthdate. However, in those circumstances where the sound of a price matches the sound of the shopper's name, say the price and the shopper's name in the same sentence.

For this effect, unlike with the getting-in-line effect I described at the start of this chapter, either first name or last name will do and it works as well with married as with unmarried men and women.

RIMinders

- Appeal to an almost universal consumer drive to care about those less able to care for themselves, such as children and pets.
- Highlight allegiances to country and family as selling points.
- If your target audience is politically conservative, emphasize national brands over house brands and avoid stocking just-released products.
- Congratulate your tightwad customers on how carefully they shop, giving them specific examples.
- To increase shoppers' aspirational purchases, praise the shoppers, even if this requires you to exaggerate somewhat.
- To strengthen the association between an item and the shopper's values system, ask the shopper to handwrite their name as part of the purchase process.
- Whenever the shopper appears willing to allow time to make a choice, encourage them to do so in terms of the shopper's distinctive system of values.
- In those circumstances where the sound of a price matches the sound of the shopper's name, say the price and the shopper's name in the same sentence.
- Remember that a shopper may consciously or subconsciously choose not to understand information you give them.

4

Habits

Researchers at University of Pennsylvania and McGill University[41] looked into the story behind the bankruptcy of grocery retailer Super Fresh. A contributing factor, so went the story, was the retailer eliminating certain slow sellers from the shelves. By the time the retailer realized how important those deleted items were to the shoppers, the shoppers had taken their habitual business elsewhere.

A profitability maxim for the small to midsize retailer is, "Don't fall in love with your inventory." Turn your slow sellers into cash, it's said. If necessary, lower the selling price to below what you originally paid for the items. Free up the shelf space and the money so you can use it on high turnover merchandise.

But with Super Fresh, those slow-selling items were serving a function other than making money on their own. They were reassuring customers that, if they needed the items, this was the place to go for them. Customers were in the habit of finding those items at the store. Because this habit was disrupted, the customers were peeved.

When you accommodate your customers' habits, their money is buying the type of happiness associated with the calmness which arises from predictability.

Georgia State University researchers[42] find that repeat purchasing is only one among a group of habits consumers can form in interactions with

41

retailers. Others include the rituals a person follows when seeking low-margin items, buying an item offered at a discount, and returning products.

Habits can be deep-seated. I once served on a team tasked with helping the State of California prison system predict how well men being considered for parole would do if released. As in consumer psychology, the challenge is to move beyond describing and understanding human behavior into educated guesses about what will happen in the future.

A joke I was told while working on the prison project nicely highlights a principle of consumer behavior:

Sitting before the parole board, the inmate is asked, "What is the first thing you'll do if we release you to the community?"

"I'll build the biggest bomb I can and blow up this place!"

Based on that answer, the board promptly turns down the man's bid for parole, telling him, "We'd like you to rethink and revise that decision. In twelve months, we'll again consider releasing you."

Each year, the inmate appears before the board, each time he's asked, "What is the first thing you'll do if we release you to the community?," he answers, "I'll build the biggest bomb I can and blow up this place!," and the parole board members recommend he develop a better plan.

But finally, one year the answer is dramatically different. The man says, "When I get out of prison, the first thing I'll do is to find a job as an accountant, making use of the thorough training I've received while incarcerated here. I realize that because of my felony record, it will be a challenge to become a Certified Public Accountant, but I shall persevere. In any case, my research has shown me that there is a demand for talented accountants. My instructors have told me I am especially talented, so I fully expect to be very successful financially."

Highly impressed, one of the parole board members asks, "What will you do with all that money?"

"To begin to compensate for the damage my crimes have inflicted on society, I'll contribute to a range of charities. But I'll always be sure I save enough to support my wife, my children, and my aging parents. I'm confident there will be sufficient funds for all that and more."

"And then what?," asks another board member.

"I'll *buy* the biggest bomb I can and blow up this place."

There is substantial inertia in human behavior. Prison inmates, consumers, and retailers change. Still, the best single predictor of future behavior is past behavior.

Researchers at University of Bonn[43] presented each of their study participants a set of dirty dishes with instructions to wash the dinnerware. Then the researchers did this a second time, and then a third time. The dishes varied in the amount of food on them from the first to the second to the third load. The experimenters were watching what difference this made in the hand washing techniques.

It turned out that the amount of soil made no difference. In each case, the study participant exhibited a habitual routine, using the same amount of water, detergent, and scrubbing effort. The dishes that started out dirtiest ended up under-washed, and the dishes starting out cleanest were over-washed.

Nourish the in-store habits which create purchase opportunities benefiting both the shopper and you. To maintain good will with your customers, tolerate the other habits and rituals which do little or no harm.

For instance, have you noticed how some shoppers will complain and complain about a product or service that seems ideally suited to the shopper's needs and desires, and then after all the complaining and what seems to be arguing with the salesperson, the shopper will go right ahead and buy the offering?

Other shoppers come into your store asking for a specific product and brand, but before buying it, as they'll end up doing, they want to hear about at least a few alternatives, as if to convince themselves they're making the right decision.

And then there are those customers who, even if a sample is available, refuse to buy a product until they can take a new one out of the packaging and run their hands over it. Except once they do make the purchase decision, they want nothing to do with the item they've soiled, insisting on you getting them an unopened package.

Some shopping rituals have their origins before birth, being hardwired in as the brain developed in the womb.

Right-handed people—constituting the large majority of most stores' customers—are more likely to buy items which are displayed in a way the items can be easily picked up with the right hand. This is true when you encourage shoppers to pick up the items. It's also true when you're only showing the item to the prospective purchaser, such as pictured in an ad or demonstrated in front of the person.

Researchers from Brigham Young University and University of Michigan[44] prepared for their experiment by creating ads which oriented to the right or the left the parts of the illustration most directly related to usage. This included handles on mugs and the placement of forks and spoons. When the orientation was to the right for a product people otherwise liked, the motivation to possess the product became even greater.

Notice that this means the more effective ad shows a mirror image of the setup for a right-handed person to use the product. The consumer is looking at the ad, so what would be closest to the consumer's right hand will have been to the left of a person whose image faces us in the ad.

For an appreciation of how this applies to in-store demonstrations of a product, think how confusing it can be when the dance instructor faces you while teaching a new move. The instructor might turn her back to you for the demonstration so that when she lifts her right arm, you know to lift your right arm, not your left arm. If facing you, the instructor does best to lift her left arm while giving you verbal instructions to lift your right arm.

When the salesperson faces the shopper while demonstrating usage of a product with the intent of having the shopper imagine usage, left becomes right while right becomes left.

People are born carrying the habit of associating a gentle smile with a desire to consume. Remember to smile on the sales floor. What distinguishes a flirtatious leer from a gracious smile might differ among cultures, but across cultures, a gracious smile helps you achieve your retail business goals. I'll first make that point by recalling a snippet of dialogue from the Academy Award-nominated 2009 movie "Invictus."

The movie's story line is of South African president Nelson Mandela guiding his nation's citizens toward reconciliation after the long pain of apartheid. In one scene, President Mandela's aide is giving instructions to the security detail who will guard the president's safety at a rugby match where many white participants have been conditioned into the habit of hating the new president. The aide instructs the security detail to maintain smiles, saying it is important to smile at the people you are asking to move.

Retailer, often you're asking people to move in their thinking and their behavior. So smile.

Even when not in-born, habits can be firmly embedded in the personality because they were introduced early in life as the child watched peers shop and was coached by parents and shopkeepers the child trusted:

The man enters the furniture store with a woman who appears to be his wife, a boy who appears to be their preteen son, and an older woman who could be the mother of one of the couple. When the salesperson approaches the four, the man shakes his head vigorously and says something to the boy in a language the salesperson doesn't understand.

"My father does not want to buy anything," says the boy. But the quartet then proceed to look carefully at the merchandise, with the man and two women chattering continually and the boy listening attentively. Finally, the boy walks toward the salesperson and, with eyes looking down, says, "My father wants to know what discount you will give him on the furniture over there."

This begins a negotiating session between the salesperson and the father, with the boy serving as interpreter. The session ends with the man agreeing to purchase a complete bedroom set.

How did this happen, and what are the lessons for other retailers?

The salesperson realized that the negotiating partner was the man. For successful negotiations, identify the decision makers.

The "what discount you will give him" wording was a cue that the man considered negotiating to be an essential part of purchasing this type of item. Respect shopper rituals.

The salesperson replied to the request for a discount by pointing out how the value of that item justified the full price. Redirecting from price to value eases a shopper's demand for a discount.

When the man—through his son—kept insisting on a discount, the salesperson hesitated before each reply. Researchers at University of Maryland[45] found that during the back and forth of negotiating a purchase price, the shopper will feel better about the final decision if the retailer waits a while before responding with an okay or a counteroffer during each round.

And when the salesperson concluded that the degree of discount requested by the customer was not realistic, the salesperson said to the boy, "Please tell your father that if he is not able to afford this furniture set, I've another set that is at the price your father desires." The instant the son finished interpreting, the father agreed to the salesperson's final offer. The words "not able to afford" called up the shopper's pride, which triggered in that shopper another habitual response.

If you see a prospective purchaser swallowing hard during negotiations, you could take this to mean they're gagging on the price of the item. However, researchers at Northwestern University[46] find that the hard swallow might better be interpreted as the prospect drooling over the possibility of purchase. When that's the case, let your selling continue to take wing rather than assume you need to descend to a lower price point.

In one study, the researchers showed a group of men photographs of physically attractive women and asked these men to decide which one they'd prefer to take out on a date if ever given the opportunity. A matching group of men were asked to think about getting a haircut at the barber. Although we might consider the first group the fantasy condition and the second group the boring-life condition, the researchers were aiming for something else: They considered the first group as developing more of a mating goal than the second group.

Once this difference was produced, all the men in both groups were asked to look at images of high-end sports cars while hosting in their mouths the type of cotton rolls a patient might encounter in the dental chair. The objective was to measure any differences in amount of salivation.

Sure enough, the men in the mating goal group salivated more when viewing the sports car images than did those in the haircut group.

Thinking about purchasing mouth-watering foods could fill a cotton roll to overflowing. Those effects can spread to anything associated with the mouth-watering foods. A mouth-watering sports car is operating on the brain in the same sort of way as the mouth-watering food. The effect is greatest when customers feel they have relatively low psychological power. This brings us back to the retailing negotiations. When a customer perceives they're in a weaker position, the repeated swallowing could mean they're unconsciously expecting the purchase to give them more influence.

This study illustrates a most fundamental type of habit-building—classical conditioning. You do remember Ivan Pavlov and how when he paired the sound of a bell with feeding a dog, pretty soon the bell caused the dog to salivate?

I admit it threatens the dignity of your customers to consider them as experimental animals like Pavlov's dog.. Still, your shoppers make many purchase decisions without much thought, and in these low-involvement decisions, they are influenced by principles of classical conditioning.

Researchers at University of British Columbia[47] presented study participants with a picture of a pen at the same time music was played. Some people were shown a blue pen, while the others were shown a beige pen. Half of the number of people in each group heard music previously qualified as pleasant to listen to, while the others listened to certifiably unpleasant music. The participants were then asked to select the blue or the beige pen.

Those who had heard the pleasant music selected the color pen they'd seen about 80% of the time. Those who had heard the unpleasant music selected the pen they'd seen about 30% of the time.

- Classical conditioning works best when the shopper is not already familiar with the items, so it could be especially helpful when introducing new brands in habitually-purchased product categories.
- You'll pair pleasant sensations with the brand or item you want the shopper to prefer. The sensations could come from music, colors, sounds, and/or fragrances you've reason to believe the shopper will find to be highly pleasant. With certain sensations, you can do the pairing in your advertising, and with certain sensations, you can do it in-store.
- The effect is strongest when you show the package or a picture of the item and then immediately follow it with the pleasant sensation. It also works to present the two at the same time or to present the pleasant sensation first, but the effect is not as strong.
- Classical conditioning nudges the shopper rather than controls the shopper. Remember that about 30% of the people in the pen study

did select the option paired with the unpleasant music. It appears their preference for the color trumped their feelings about the tunes.

Completing a purchase can itself become a cue for making subsequent purchases. Consider what happened in a study conducted by researchers at Yale University, Duke University, and Carnegie Mellon University:[48]

Some study participants were invited to buy a CD that had been previously judged as appealing to people like the participants. The rest of the participants were invited, instead, to buy a light bulb. Yes, the butt of so many "how many does it take" jokes. A lowly light bulb. As you might expect, a higher percentage of the CD group than the light bulb group decided to make the purchase.

Next, all participants—regardless of what they'd been offered before and whether or not they made a purchase—were invited to buy a key chain. Shopping momentum evidenced itself. A higher percentage from the CD group than from the light bulb group decided to buy the key chain, and those in the light bulb group who did make the purchase were more likely to buy the key chain than those who turned down the light bulb offer.

Consumer psychologists call this short-term habit a "flow state" or "purchase momentum." The flow state includes decisiveness in buying decisions, a playful willingness to expand the range of products considered, a hesitation to discontinue the process of shopping, and a distorted sense of time.

An application of this for your store is in how you frame quantity-dependent price discounts. Two of the possibilities are in the format:
- 20% off if you buy at least five packages.
- 20% off. Limit five packages per customer.
   What's the effect of those on the number of items purchased?
- When customers are required to buy a minimum quantity to achieve the discount, they are more motivated to purchase multiple items.
- When customers are allowed to purchase only a limited number of items at the discounted price, they are less motivated to purchase multiple items.
   Consumers live up or down to the conditions of a discount offer.

Bryant University and University of Illinois[49] researchers went beyond this to indicate that the nature of the motivation will spread to other purchase decisions during the remainder of that same shopping trip. People who buy five of the items so they can earn the discount will be more likely to buy in quantity other items on their shopping list—whether or not those items are discounted. Customers who stopped at buying five items because they don't get a discount beyond that quantity become less likely to supersize purchases of other items on the shopping list.

Don't exploit purchase momentum—such as in children or people with a compulsive buying disorder. But allow customers to both build your profitability and build their enjoyment from shopping with you by maintaining purchase momentum. Start your shoppers saying yes. Begin with purchases the shopper is most likely to agree to. Use one of the oldest selling tactics in the world—the foot-in-the-door technique. FITD consists of starting out with such a small request that the shopper is very likely to say yes and then using this yes as a base for presenting a series of larger requests.

Especially respect the power of habits when those habits occur subconsciously. Some years ago, I conducted a two-day "Retail Profitability Tactics" workshop with a set of business advisors from the Los Angeles Regional Small Business Development Center Network. The objective of the workshop was to equip the business advisors to help their retailer clients make more money.

The evening between the two days of intensive training, a couple of the business advisors supplemented their retailing knowledge by shopping at an IKEA store in the area. Their little trip worked out well for me because they were able to provide a compelling example of a tactic I presented the second day. Well, actually, it was a compelling example of a failure to use the tactic I was discussing. My topic was the value of giving each customer a clear sense of progress through the purchase process to fit the customer's habitual expectations. "Sound off," I said, by which I meant to make some pleasant noise.

But for those two business advisors, the sound was off: At the cash/wrap, the pair of shoppers experienced an unsettled feeling. There was no sound accompanying the completion of the purchase. No sound of a cash register. No acknowledgement from the cashier, who had moved on to the next customer. No sound of a package going into a bag. As the shoppers learned, this last one was because the store charged a fee for a bag.

Sounds from the shopping experience can burn themselves into the brains of consumers. Since some of the last sounds the shopper hears before leaving the store are those associated with making the purchase, those sounds are especially important. We want customers to come back soon and often, so we want them to take away pleasing memories.

Reward the purchaser with sound effects they'll find pleasant. This protects the good will you've built to that point.

Give sounds of confirmation as the transaction progresses. A brief series of tones tells the customer that completion of the sale is getting closer. On the other hand, silence breeds annoying uncertainty.

Then top it off with the most pleasing sound of all. Say thank you.

At the other extreme from habits carried out subconsciously are those exercised intentionally by the shopper in ways that could undercut your profitability. Ascertain motivations for the habits:

As the shopkeeper spots the ten-year-old boy coming in the door, he says to a customer, "I know this is the first time you've been in my store. I want you to see probably the dumbest kid you will ever encounter in your life."

While the customer watches, the shopkeeper opens the cash register, takes out some money, places a dollar bill in one open palm and two quarters in the other, and says to the kid, "Okay, which do you want?"

The boy hesitates for a moment before pointing to the hand with the two quarters. The shopkeeper shakes his head, chuckles, hands him the coins, and returns the dollar bill to the register. The boy picks up items from the shelves, comes to the counter, plunks down the two quarters, and pulls more coins out of his pocket to pay for the rest that's due.

This entire episode without the kid saying one word. Nothing.

The customer who'd watched all this is intrigued. She quickly makes her purchase and follows the boy out the door. When they're both on the sidewalk, she asks, "I'm wondering, why'd you choose two quarters instead of the dollar bill?"

"The day I take the dollar, that's the day I stop getting fifty cents every time I come by."

That kid was far from dumb. The shopkeeper was on to something, too, even if not realizing it consciously. The boy had become a reliable repeat customer.

50

Because of the stability of habits—whether inborn, acquired over time, or stimulated by the retailer—lead your customers through changes gradually.

Every retail business changes. It might be a change in your mix of products or services because of a need to reduce inventory or opportunities to expand your offerings. It could be a change in business location or format to better meet the preferences of your target markets. You might be changing staffing in ways which will be noticed by your regular shoppers.

Leading your customers gradually reduces the possibilities that you'll disrupt loyalty. Determine where you want to end up, and if this ending point is quite different from where you are now, introduce intermediate steps to the degree possible. If you currently sell paint and you want to end up adding draperies, consider introducing wallpaper first. If you plan to phase out your entire stock of draperies, reduce the product assortment for a while before eliminating the product category completely.

There are some changes where intermediate steps are unrealistic. If you want to close down your current store and move the whole operation across town, it wouldn't work to open up a store halfway across town for a while as an intermediate step. Here the principle becomes "Ease your customers into making the changes." Is it realistic to keep the old location open for a while after opening up the new location? Can you announce the change at least a month in advance of making it and show a map of how to get from the old store to the new store? Can you post large drawings of the new store in the old store?

Customers like some changes. It makes shopping less tedious. How hellish it would be to endure the same routine forever. We all like variety. People buy more jelly beans when they're offered an assortment of colors. This is true even if all the different-colored jelly beans taste exactly the same. Variety stimulates the shopper. That's why surveys find that somewhere between 65% and 85% of customers who start shopping elsewhere say they were satisfied with the prior retailer. They wanted a little change of scene.

It's the large changes that can lead to customer discomfort. You can make an extreme change seem like a moderate change by clearly pointing out ways in which the new is similar to the old. When introducing a new product or brand, work in phrases like, "the same way as with the brand you're accustomed to using," and, "once you do this a few times, it will be as second nature to you as what you've been doing up to now."

Store loyalty is indeed itself a habit of special interest to retailers. You'll want to minimize switching costs for shoppers who decide to change from another store to shopping with you. At the same time, you'd like to maximize costs to shoppers who are considering making a switch from your store to that of a competing retailer.

Switching costs exert a stronger influence than does customer satisfaction on whether a consumer will continue to patronize a business. There are three sorts of switching costs in retailer-to-consumer and business-to-business sales:

- **Procedural.** The loss of time and labor. Consumers are uncertain how things will work out with the new retailer. It takes time to gather information and mental effort to analyze it. The retail consumer asks, "How difficult will it be for me to change my habits, such as quickly locating the items I regularly buy, if I shop at the other store?" The business consumer asks, "How hard will it be for me to set up new accounts if I change retail suppliers?" A retailer wanting to keep current customers can increase procedural switching costs by satisfying a broader range of the customer's needs.

- **Financial.** The loss of money or money equivalents. "Will I lose frequent shopper points, quantity purchase discounts, or deposits if I switch now?" "Are there deposits I'll need to make to do business with a different retailer?" Financial switching costs are higher when the retailer has multilevel loyalty programs and purchase protection plans.

- **Relational.** The loss of a steady identity which comes from association with the retailer. Customers of small to midsize retailers enjoy seeing store staff they recognize and who recognize them, or even call them by name. A barrier to switching is the consumer's discomfort with having to become acquainted with a new set of store staff. In addition, people often augment their self-identity using the personalities of the stores they frequent. For this reason, changing stores can be psychologically disruptive. If your customer has done business with you for a long time, the relational switching costs are higher. When you continue to offer distinctive products and services, you're building resistances against your customers abandoning you.

Throughout it all when dealing with habits, stay aware of how ready, willing, and able your target audience is to make any of the changes you're expecting.

In the late 1960s, as the support ship R/V Lulu was lowering the deep-sea exploration submarine Alvin into the ocean off the coast of Massachusetts, the cradle support cables broke. Because the hatch on Alvin had not yet been completely closed, Alvin began taking on water.

The three crew members quickly escaped with no more than a single sprained ankle among them. But, alas, there was insufficient time to extricate the crew's bologna sandwiches. The lunch and Alvin itself gently sank to 5,000 feet below sea level. Almost one mile down.

It was nearly one year before the submarine could be retrieved. Understandably, the bologna sandwiches were soggy. But how tasty were they?, the scientists, being scientists, wondered. Quite salty and otherwise quite fine was the conclusion from sampling.

This led to the next question: At 5,000 feet below, you wouldn't expect fish or crabs to be around to nibble the bologna. However, what about bacteria? Cold sea water can be an excellent preservative, but if you leave bologna sandwiches in salt water for a year on your kitchen counter, the bacteria will have had a feast.

The scientists' answer to the question: At that depth, there are no bacteria. Life has its limits. Any bacteria managing to paddle down that deep would promptly die.

This was in 1969. Over the decades, the original answer has been declared dead wrong. Or more accurately, wrong about dead. There are plenty of bacteria and other life forms at 5,000 feet down and beyond. The current salty answer regarding the highly-seasoned sandwiches came from John Parkes, a geomicrobiologist at Cardiff University: "It was just that at that depth the bugs had never seen a bologna sandwich before."

They hadn't physically evolved to consume bologna. And your shoppers may not have intellectually and emotionally evolved to consume highly novel products, services, or experiences falling outside their habitual rituals. What you're selling could be sitting there perfectly preserved for a year with still no bites.

To sell well, accommodate the power and perseverance of habits.

RIMinders

- Tolerate shopper habits—for example, the refusal of some shoppers to purchase the first alternative shown to them—which are bothersome, but do little or no harm.
- At the start of negotiating with a shopper, determine their negotiating rituals, such as how the individual makes counteroffers.
- To increase the appeal of an item, present the item and then immediately present music, colors, sounds, or fragrances which shoppers are in the habit of finding to be pleasant.
- Start your shoppers saying yes. Begin with purchases the shopper is most likely to agree to. Even having a shopper nod yes builds that shopper's buying momentum.
- "20% off if you buy at least five packages" earns retailers more money than "20% off. Limit five packages per customer."
- Give sounds of confirmation as the sales transaction progresses. Then top it off with the most pleasing sound of all. Say thank you.
- Lead your customers through changes gradually. Determine where you want to end up, and if this ending point is quite different from where you are now, aim to introduce a series of intermediate steps.
- Stay aware of how ready, willing, and able your target audience is to make any of the changes you're expecting.

5

Familiarity

~~

Researchers at University of Southern Brittany[50] observed customers who were asking for advice about selecting an MP3 player in a retail store. Unbeknownst to the shoppers, some of the salespeople had been given instructions which you might consider to be rather strange: Subtly mimic the shopper. If the shopper uses their hands while talking, you do a little of the same. If the shopper paces back and forth, you pace back and forth a bit. Is the shopper talking softly while avoiding direct glances? Then that's what you'll do, but subtly.

In other cases, the salesperson was not instructed to mimic the shopper.

What difference did it make? About 79% of the shoppers in the subtly-mimicked group ended up purchasing an MP3 player. Among those who were not mimicked, about 62% made the buy. In addition, the customers whose salespersons had been instructed to subtly mimic the shopper rated the salesperson and the store itself more favorably when asked afterwards.

The researchers explain this "chameleon effect" by saying that having someone subtly mirror your behavior makes that other person more familiar to you. This relaxes barriers to trust, so you comply with the person's requests. Such as buying an MP3 player recommended by the subtle mimic.

A related explanation, offered by another set of research findings, is at the level of brain waves. One distinctive tool you have in face-to-face selling is the ability to reflect each shopper's brain activity. When communication between two people is at its best, the brain waves of the two people actually come to have similarities. Along with this, the listener—such as the retail salesperson—begins to anticipate where the speaker—the prospective customer—is going next in their thoughts, and can therefore better influence those thoughts.

The enhanced understanding of the shopper boosts your powers in guiding the shopper's purchase decisions. It works best with customers you already know, and there are significant differences among salespeople in the ability to do this sort of mindreading. But research findings do suggest ways to get better at it.

- Listen carefully not only to the words the shopper is using, but also to their tone of voice. Watch the shopper's gestures and facial expressions. Figure out how the signals all go together so you can get good at reading the brain and mimicking the shopper subtly.
- Be aware of when you're in sync. The researchers say you'll experience distinctive gut feelings letting you know you're now tuned in.
- It's okay to redirect the shopper's thinking. However, don't suddenly interrupt, such as by finishing off the shopper's sentences. When you're reading somebody's mind, tipping your hand makes it seem creepy, causing the shopper to instantly become guarded.

Consumers of every age are attracted by familiarity. Young children love repetition in television programming. Esteemed shows like "Dora the Explorer" and "Blue's Clues" invariably followed a strict formula. The developmental psychology explanation is that repetition gives children a sense of security.

Many of the programs targeted to adults also have a highly formulaic format. To be sure, "Been there, done that" easily makes people's lists of top ten trite phrases, suggesting that consumers avoid revisiting experiences they've already had. In the prior chapter, I talked about the advantages of different-colored jelly beans, and in Chapter 6, I'll build my case further for you stimulating shoppers with variety. Still, people will sometimes read the same book a number of times, watch the same movie repeatedly, or go back to the same place and engage in the same activities.

Researchers at American University, University of Arizona, and Northwestern University[51] mused on why. Analyzing in-depth interviews with consumers in the U.S. and in New Zealand, the assessment team identified a set of reasons for the appeal in being there and doing it again: Experiencing familiar sensations in new ways. Refreshing the old memories. Seeking out details missed last time because of the limitations of human attention. Added pleasure in being there while friends encounter a movie or a travel destination that the consumer previously enjoyed.

You can attract shoppers by offering a never-ending panoply of new experiences. But always temper the change with comfortable repetition. Enable shoppers to revisit the already done. The State Fair visitors may rarely be certain what additional item will be offered up fried this year by the midway retailers, but they can always take comfort in knowing there will be fried something. Well, comfort at least until they go on the roller coaster.

The yearning for familiarity in stressful times has implications for where your retail business might consider locating. Researchers from Imperial College London and Toronto's Sunnybrook Health Sciences Centre[52] surveyed more than 3,000 visitors and outpatients at a total of seven hospitals. About 70% of their respondents said that retail businesses in a hospital added great value to the consumers' experiences under difficult circumstances. Around the same percentage said that a retailer's presence at a hospital would make it more likely they'd purchase from that business at another location and speak positively to others about the retailer.

What types of stores did the visitors and patients want? The types of places you could browse in to find familiar items: Clothing, electronics, books.

Wherever you're operating your retail business, also aim for the right amount of familiarity in the merchandise you offer. What consumer experts call a "prototype brand" on your store shelves or racks carries the name and label design best known by consumers in your target markets in that product or service category. For peanut butter, the prototype might be Skippy. Prototype electronics brands have included Sony, Samsung, and Apple. From the geographical angle, the prototype brand of laundry detergent might be Tide in Milwaukee, All Free in San Francisco, and Ala in Buenos Aries. For beer, it's been Budweiser in America and Heineken in the Netherlands.

A "copycat brand" you choose to carry in your store aims to imitate the appearance of the prototype brand. Copycat brands can sell well. However, the type of copycat you carry should be based on the proximity of the prototype brand. Distinguish among low-, moderate-, and high-similarity copycats, depending on how much the package design and brand name resemble the prototype's.

If you don't carry the prototype brand in your store, you'll do best having high-similarity copycats. On the other hand, if you stock the prototype brand adjacent to the copycats, you'll do best carrying moderate-similarity copycats.

From a shopper psychology perspective, the second strategy is better. By stocking both the prototype and copycat, you offer alternatives, and the power to choose does attract shoppers. When the copycat is physically close to the prototype, the shopper's mind attributes positive characteristics of the prototype to the copycat. As a retailer, you'll be hitchhiking onto the strong images prototypes carry. Their manufacturers devote massive amounts of marketing support to maintaining top-of-mind awareness.

Yet when a prototype is close by, a high-similarity copycat implies trickery to the shopper and so arouses suspiciousness. This is especially likely if you have charts in ads or on store signs which compare characteristics, features, or benefits of the copycat and the prototype. The moderate-similarity copycat doesn't arouse this degree of consumer suspiciousness. The person realizes they can easily tell the difference in package design, so won't be tricked.

Shoppers find comfort in being with brands they've known well for a long time. Consumer psychologists talk about the "mere exposure effect." Shoppers tend to have more favorable attitudes toward something they've seen before. In a set of studies, Southern Methodist University[53] researchers lied to study participants in telling them the participants had seen brands previously. The people who were convinced they had seen the brands before showed the same sorts of favorable attitudes as if they actually had.

Copycats work well because of the mere exposure effect, and as long as product or service performance meets customers' expectations, the copycat can become their personal prototype.

The principle of familiarity drives the language to use in selling well. On September 7, 2010, a front-page article in the *Baltimore Sun* carried the headline "Opposing votes limn difference in race." Well, at least a few of the newspaper's readers that day reacted as if they'd like to rip the editors limn from limn. Whoops, I mean limb from limb, which is pronounced the same way.

As to the definition, limn shares its word root with illuminate and means to give clear, sharp detail. The headline meant that a set of opposing votes portrayed differences between the current electoral candidates in clear, sharp detail.

But those upset readers of the headline didn't know what "limn" meant. They were irritated at the *Baltimore Sun* for creating an unnecessary difficulty. One reader opined, "To put a word like 'limn' in the headline for the lead article on the front page of this newspaper seems to me to be unbelievably arrogant and patronizing. Could the headline writer not have fashioned a head around the word 'illuminate,' 'delineate' or 'depict'? Perhaps then more readers would not only understand what the article is about but actually might want to read it."

Off-base on two counts. First, the *Sun*'s headline writer said he chose the word not to impress with his vocabulary, but because he needed a shorter word for "show" in a one-column space. Second, classic research by psychologist Edward Wheeler Scripture found that a bit of puzzlement in a headline—whether for a newspaper article or newspaper ad—increases interest in reading what follows. In an 1895 book, Dr. Scripture used his studies' findings to suggest putting commercial notices upside down in order to attract attention. I'll return to this theme briefly later in this chapter when I present you a few puzzles and then again in Chapter 6 when I discuss mystery ads.

Using a fancy word also can subtly add to your impression of distinctiveness or exclusivity in a positive way. A two-store California retailer named themselves Limn to fit their merchandising of sharply designed high-end home furniture, lighting, and accessories.

Now that you know what limn means, I can recommend to you that you limn for your special attention any words that your target audiences are likely not to understand correctly at first viewing or first hearing. Give each of those words clear, sharp detail as you create your marketing copy and selling scripts. Then decide for each of the words if it will arouse useful interest in your intended message or create a distracting kerfuffle. Whoops, maybe I should say, instead, create a distracting fuss.

Or a distracting irritation. Please recall my measurement units example from Chapter 1. Those consumers presented with a comparison between a warranty of 84 months and 108 months perceived the difference to be larger than did consumers presented with a comparison between seven years and nine years. A similar effect was seen with the measurements of a dining room table (inches versus feet) and merchandise delivery times (days versus weeks).

If you want to leave with the shopper the impression of higher magnitude, quote in smaller units. If you want to make things seem smaller, as with treatment duration, quote in larger units. If the magnitude indicates degree of benefit, go for larger numerals. If a longer duration will be perceived by the shopper as indicating greater personal sacrifice, use the phrasing with a smaller numeral. Describe a self-improvement program in which the shopper would be highly involved as, "This will take one year," instead of, "This will take twelve months."

It also works with delivery times. Let's say you need to tell the purchaser about a delay. When is it better to say, "Your product will be arriving in three weeks, not one week," and when should you use, "Your product will be arriving in 21 days instead of 7"?

If the customer is anxiously awaiting the arrival in order to start using the item, favor the first wording. In this case, the customer is looking for small. If the customer's focus is instead on, "I made the purchase then because it was a great price, but I won't be using the item right away," describe the delay in terms of days.

More recently, researchers at University of South Carolina and Virginia Tech[54] discovered a refinement to the rule: Shoppers will consider a table "4 by 5 feet" to be larger than one "48 by 60 inches" if the shopper is considering making the purchase at some indefinite point in the future, not right now. For consumers who want the table delivered today, 48 by 60 inches sounds larger than four by five feet. But people who are inquiring about possibilities will code feet as larger than inches, so "four by five feet" will be remembered by them as larger. Consumers who are gathering information for future use tend to process measurement information in terms of units rather than numbers.

The researchers uncovered this effect not only with table sizes, but also with perceptions of the time of maturity of financial products, the weight of nutrients, and the height of buildings.

All good guidance, but now back to what I said about avoiding a distracting irritation. Researchers at Ghent University[55] verified another refinement—one I'll call the "Don't Be Silly Rule for Giving Measurement Units." Start describing dining room table dimensions in millimeters or talking about warranty lengths in hours, and your shoppers will consider this odd enough to think less of the retail offering overall. They might perceive it's larger, but they won't like it as much.

When the shopper is focused on a particular dimension as highly important in the purchase, use a measurement unit the shopper is familiar with for that dimension.

Related to the mere exposure effect is the "truth effect." Repeat the benefits of a product to a shopper three times and the shopper is more likely to be convinced what you are saying is true. Effective repetition can even be in the sound of the words. Rhythmically rhyming claims in addition to being remembered better are more likely to be perceived as true than those which do not have this attribute.

Campaigning politicians and Southern Baptist ministers know the value of rhyming jingles and exhortations when appealing to the emotions. Long ago, William Shakespeare wrote the call-and-response, "In reason nothing... Something then in rhyme." The rhythm of rhymes soothes our defenses, and the repetition of sounds lends the sort of familiarity we associate with truth.

Over the years, we've heard "Oh thank heaven for 7-Eleven," Pillsbury's "Nothin' says lovin' like something from the oven," Bounty paper towels' "The quicker picker-upper," and "Call Roto-Rooter, that's the name, and away go troubles down the drain!"

The longer-form repetition works best if you repeat the product benefits, selling points, or usage instructions in different ways. When you deliver an identical message again and again and again, the shopper might come to believe it, but at some point, they also start disliking you and the product. Consumer psychologists have a name for this one, too: wear out. Wear out is more likely when the shopper is carefully evaluating what you're saying. That's why many TV ads can get away with rote repetition: Nobody's listening that carefully.

What gives the best payback for a retailer's advertising dollars when running a series of text ads, such as in a newspaper or online? Each ad should show movement forward from the prior ad. This is more effective than a campaign which repeats all the same content in each ad word-for-word. However, in each ad, mobilize the truth effect by repeating elements that relate to the theme of the campaign. Although the ads show progress, repetition drills the messages into consumers' long-term memories.

On the other hand, the familiarity of a sales pitch in the retailer's mind can operate to the disadvantage of the retailer when it's out of synch with the shopper's degree of familiarity. After years of observing retailers interacting with prospective customers, I've decided that many are too quick to believe you can get results by saying something once. The root cause isn't customer or staff stupidity. It is retailer familiarity: The retailers assume that if they themselves are highly familiar with why a certain product is good, the other party will get the message promptly.

Effective retailers repeat themselves. The benefits are due to both content and contact. When you repeat yourself, you're maintaining contact with the message recipient. You're making your presence felt, which strengthens your influence. Customers are inundated with instructions and suggestions. Repetition adds distinctiveness.

Often, a retailer can intentionally create repetition to produce the benefits of familiarity. Consumer psychologists call it "priming." To illustrate, I'll start with a question for you: Can you guess what the following sentence means?

"The haystack was important because the cloth would rip."

Researchers at State University of New York-Stony Brook, University of Minnesota, and Vanderbilt University[56] asked people to remember sentences like that, which at first hearing seem to be nonsense.

It's the sort of thing your customer might experience when they ask you a question and you assume they have knowledge they, in actuality, don't have. You'd be requiring your customer to make a guess, to fill in the blanks. The customer might say, "I don't understand what you mean. Please tell me more." But there's also a good chance they'll turn around in confusion and walk away from the sale you'd like to complete.

Sometimes it is only one word which produces all the difference. In my guessing game, I'll make a guess myself. I think that if I say to you the word "parachute," the sentence "The haystack was important because the cloth would rip" not only makes sense, but also produces a memorable mental image.

This is the sort of phenomenon we'd like to produce when answering a customer's question—an aha experience in which what you've said to the customer brings things together for them. We transform the unfamiliar into the familiar.

Another example from the research study. The sentence is "The notes were sour because the seam was split."

Again, one word can make all the difference, turning nonsense into perfect sense. In your retailing, it often will take more than one word to produce the aha experience as you explain an answer you've given to a customer. However, in this case, priming your brain with the single word "bagpipe" should do it.

The Victoria's Secret shopping bag study I presented to you in Chapter 2 is an example of how priming can influence shoppers' attitudes as well as their understandings. Recall that the women in the study were asked to carry a shopping bag for an hour as they walked around a mall. Some of the women carried a Victoria's Secret shopping bag. The rest carried a pink shopping bag with no store or brand identification. At the end of the hour, each woman returned to the research site and was asked to rate herself on a list of personality traits.

Compared to those who carried the plain bag, the women who carried the Victoria's Secret bag were more likely to rate themselves as feminine, glamorous, and physically attractive. These are characteristics associated with the Victoria's Secret store and merchandise brands.

Does this mean that giving your customers a shopping bag with your logo on it significantly strengthens their identification with your store? Well, the study design was more complicated than what I've told you so far, and those complexities shape the best ways to profitably use the findings.

Here are the two complexities:

First, each woman in the study chose whether to carry the Victoria's Secret bag or the plain bag. Therefore, one explanation for the findings is that women who choose a bag with the store brand on it are saying they want to be considered as having personality traits like the store brand. A classic philosophical question is, "Which came first, the chicken or the egg?" In this study, we can ask, "Does carrying the bag influence the shopper's personality, or does the shopper's intended personality influence the bag they select to carry?" The answer is, "It works in both directions."

Second, carrying the Victoria's Secret bag did not have an effect on all the women shoppers. Those for whom it did have the most effect were shoppers who aspired to be better in some way, but felt they couldn't do it on their own. They are the type of people who depend on brands to help them achieve their self-esteem aspirations.

For the aspirational merchandise you sell, offer branded paper bags to the customer to serve as priming cues.

Still, that's not all. There's a little more I didn't tell you, although you've probably figured it out for yourself, considering the puzzle-solving tone I've set for this chapter: If you sell merchandise like Victoria's Secret sells, there might be shoppers who prefer to conceal their purchase inside a plain paper bag while walking the mall.

Next, let's move from silky things to scavengers. Before any shopping bag gets used, product adjacencies can act as primes, perhaps in ways you don't prefer. In what area of your store do you shelve the shampoo to kill head lice? You don't carry shampoo to kill head lice? Okay, for the moment, pretend you do in order to help me make a point that's useful regardless of what product lines you carry.

It might seem that the logical place to merchandise lice-killer shampoo is adjacent to the other shampoos and the hair conditioning products. However, research findings from Northwestern University and University of Chicago[57] suggest you're better off keeping it away from there, instead stocking it in the illness remedies department.

In their study, the researchers first had participants look at an advertisement for shampoo. They wanted to evaluate the degree to which exposure to the shampoo ad would affect the participants' impressions of a related product—hair conditioners. In a previous study, the same researchers had found that thinking about mayonnaise products builds a more positive impression of related condiments, such as ketchup.

But when the ad presented to the participants was for a lice-killer shampoo, this instead led to more negative impressions of the hair conditioners. Consumers want their hair conditioners to have a pleasant sensual personality. Potions associated with killing and with bloodsuckers fail to project that personality.

In contrast, thinking about the lice-killer had no significant effect on the participants' liking of products from categories which don't depend on being pleasantly sensual in order to motivate purchase. The researchers predicted, and then confirmed, this to be true when the lice-killer shampoo was stocked next to flashlight batteries.

As we'd expect, there are variations in how consumers categorize products and therefore the strength of carryover. One gender-based example has to do with sanitary napkins. As a rule, men to a much greater extent than do women will build negative impressions of products sold next to where the sanitary napkins are shelved. Men and woman have different personality associations with that product category.

It's not only related products that imbue their shelf mates with personality. Build prestige for items you sell by displaying to your shoppers the proper contextual cues for the values your shoppers hold. Show the clothing worn, the other products used, and the sorts of physical locations that consumers associate with the people your shoppers want to be like. Do this in advertising, store displays, e-commerce pages, and to the extent you can, in what your salespeople wear and the phrases they use.

Priming is at its best whenever the retailer creates positive familiarity for the shopper. Remember from Chapter 1 how V8 juice has an advantage over Campbell's tomato juice because the V8 has a number in the name? Well, it get more complicated. Researchers at University of Florida and National University of Singapore[58] ended up asking study participants whether they'd prefer a glass of V8 or Campbell's tomato juice. But before this question, the participants had been shown an advertisement for V8. For one group of participants, the ad read, "Get a full day's supply of essential vitamins and minerals with a bottle of V8." For the other participants, the ad read, "Get a full day's supply of 4 essential vitamins and 2 minerals with a bottle of V8."

Some of the people in each group chose the tomato juice. There are people who don't like V8 or really like tomato juice, and there are people who would rebel against what they'd perceive as an effort by the experimenter to brainwash them via advertising.

However, we'd expect that more of the participants in each of the ad groups would choose V8 than would choose the tomato juice. They'd been shown an ad for V8 presenting the argument it was good. In addition, there are what psychologists call "demand characteristics." Most study participants like to help out an experimenter who is nice, and showing the ad would make the participants think the experimenter wanted them to choose the V8. When you're nice to shoppers, they're more open to suggestions you make.

But that's not the main point of my telling you about this study. Rather, my main point has to do with the fact that the people who saw the second version of the ad were even more likely to select the V8 than the tomato juice.

The only difference in the ads was the higher preference when the ad said, "4 essential vitamins and 2 minerals" instead of simply "essential vitamins and minerals." Why did this make a difference?

One good possibility is that adding the specific numbers added to the credibility of the ad. The claim of "4 essential vitamins" rings more true than just, "Essential vitamins." However, the researcher's methodology led them to another explanation: Consumers are attracted to products which use familiar numbers in their names. One way a number gains familiarity is to have it introduced subconsciously in advance. An ad which uses the numbers 4 and 2 will subconsciously generate the numbers 6 (4 plus 2) and 8 (4 times 2). A preference for V8 was created.

When you carry products which have a number in the name, the list of attributes, or the statement of benefits, the preference will be greater if you prime the consumer in advance with the mathematical operands, such as a 2 and a 20 if you're wanting the shopper to like 40 (2 times 20) or 22 (2 plus 20). The effect is so strong that consumers are more likely to choose offers which are financially less advantageous to them when the offer contains numbers which are multiples of each other. For instance, a discount of 20% off an item usually costing $40, with a 2-year warranty on the item, could draw more purchasers than a discount of 25% off that same item with that same warranty.

Show me a tree with spreading branches—or even a picture of a large tree—at the entrance to your store and I become more likely to consider the items in your store to be healthy, research says. Trees generally prime shoppers to interpret what comes next as more healthy.

There is, however, a wrinkle in all this: Broad individual differences among consumers. When I see a tree bearing branches and blossoms, I've the subconscious urge to breathe deeply. There are people for whom this will be a prime to buy allergy meds.

The image of the tree might bring to mind strength, in which case the consumer is moved closer to buying the strongest detergent on the shelf. Or as I look at the shade directly under the tree, maybe I'll start thinking, "Oh my gosh! I forget to water my lawn this morning," thereby diverting my attention toward buying a sprinkler system. That's less useful to the retailer who devotes shelf space to strong detergents rather than sprinkler systems.

Primes are stronger when presented as a set, stimulating the brain from different angles. If we're aiming for the impression of healthy as a purchasing prime, we'll show not only the image of a tree, but also images of people exercising and of nutritious food.

The shopper's body movements can serve as primes. In certain situations, shoppers become more likely to make a purchase after reading text—such as on signage and packaging—in narrow adjacent columns. The reason this is said to work: In order to read the text, a shopper needs to slowly nod their head up and down, and this sign of yes subconsciously produces even more positive evaluations of products the customer already likes.

Researchers at Erasmus University, Loughborough University, and BI Norwegian Business School[59] report that when a consumer pulls their arm toward themselves, the consumer becomes more likely to purchase short-term pleasure over longer-term benefits. Have the restaurant patron lift the water glass to mouth to quaff the contents instead of drinking through a straw, and the potential for ordering dessert climbs. What's even stranger is that when a shopper uses a basket instead of a cart in a grocery store, the shopper is almost seven times as likely to purchase candy bars rather than fruit as a snack.

Over our lifetimes, our brains subconsciously associate pulling our arms toward ourselves with acquiring pleasurable objects. For the adult consumer, pulling the arm toward the body activates subconscious expectations of short-term pleasure, and the arm pullers look to fulfill those expectations.

Shoppers can prime each other toward the sense of well-being which allows us to sell well. Even when the people in your store don't interact directly with each other, their emotional states influence each other. University of Queensland[60] researchers observed positive and negative feelings displayed by shoppers in retail environments moment-to-moment. Not only did a general emotional tone spread, but if one shopper changed from negative to positive or in the opposite direction, other shoppers tracked along with their own behavioral evidence of emotions. All this, in turn, was found to affect intentions to purchase items at the store and intentions to return to the store for future purchases.

Thus, moving a shopper from being disgruntled to being pleased increases your profitability from that customer and also for other shoppers in the store at the time who observe the interactions.

The effect is quick and often below the level of conscious awareness. Remember how in the prior chapter I touted the value of a gentle smile in your voice and on your face? Researchers at University of California-San Diego and University of Michigan[61] offered thirsty participants in a study a serving of a beverage. Along with this, some of the participants were exposed to a brief image of a frowning face and some to a brief image of a smiling face. The exposure was so brief that any notice of the emotion would almost surely be subconscious. In addition, the exposure of the emotion-laden face occurred along with the person being shown an emotionally neutral face for a long enough time to be consciously perceived.

The thirsty people shown the smiling face didn't report feeling much different from those shown the frowning face. However, those shown the smiling face poured more beverage from the offered pitcher into their cup, drank more from their cup, and were willing to pay about twice as much for the beverage. A smile—even one so brief as to have no conscious effect—made for more motivated consumers.

Notice, though, that the experiment was done with people who were already thirsty. As with the classical conditioning effects of pen color selection I discussed in Chapter 4, emotional contagion nudges purchase behavior, but doesn't dictate it.

The infection of emotions spreads from staff to shoppers, too, and among staff. So smile often when greeting customers. And smile often when building teamwork with your employees.

To be sure, there are retailing situations in which a smile is all wrong: If a customer is distraught, and a smile would make you look uncaring. If you're delivering corrective discipline to a staff member, and a smile would make what you're saying seem unimportant. Or when a prolonged smile threatens to make you look simply dopey.

Primes should be subtle, never overwhelming or overly obvious. Suppose the salesperson in the MP3 player study I described at the start of this chapter had been obvious in mimicking the shopper. The tactic would have backfired, probably with the prospective purchaser feeling ridiculed. Shoppers who are aware of priming are more likely to feel manipulated, setting off rebellion. Delivering the prompts below the level of awareness makes the primes more influential over a shopper's behavior. Subconscious primes result in fewer counterarguments.

Early planting of the idea helps, too. A subconscious influence is a seed inside the brain, and seeds take at least a little time to sprout. Coupons presented at the store entrance drive up sales much more than do coupons available in the aisles of stores. By extension, if you deliver the coupons to the consumer a few days before they shop with you, the coupons are more likely to generate redemption desires.

Because of the power of priming, we retailing professionals are obliged to use it ethically. Those who carefully follow my RIMtailing blog at www. rimtailing.blogspot.com may recall that the annual Ig Noble Awards are given out by the *Annals of Improbable Research* for studies which come across as odd enough to usually draw a chuckle. Unlike the Nobel Prizes, which are awarded with formal pomp in Oslo City Hall in Norway and Stockholm Concert Hall in Sweden, the Ig Noble Award ceremony is held in the Sanders Theatre at Harvard University and includes Miss Sweetie Poo, always an eight-year-old girl selected for that year who begins loudly and repetitively chanting, "Please stop. I'm bored," at any recipient whose speech exceeds the allotted time limit.

The 2013 Psychology prize was awarded to Laurent Bègue, Oulmann Zerhouni, Brad Bushman, Baptiste Subra, and Medhi Ourabah. They were honored for their study, published in the May 2013 issue of *British Journal of Psychology*, titled "Beauty Is in the Eye of the Beer Holder: People Who Think They Are Drunk Also Think They Are Attractive."

Please note the "who think they are drunk," not, "who are drunk." The study participants—none of them college students—who either imbibed a fair amount of alcohol or were primed to believe they'd imbibed a fair amount of alcohol when they actually hadn't tended to rate themselves as brighter, funnier, and more attractive than did those who did not consume the alcohol and were told they hadn't.

The less bright, less funny, less attractive counterpart to the levity of this Ig Noble Award is that our customers might use the products and services we sell them to justify bad behavior. I once took on the consulting assignment of maximizing the payoffs from a program to reduce alcohol abuse among teenagers. One of our findings was that, at teen parties, boys who got intoxicated often had the objective of relaxing themselves to improve their sexual performance and girls who got intoxicated often had the objective of providing themselves an excuse for taboo sexual activity.

We can do only so much to protect customers from themselves. But especially when it comes to young people, I suggest we retailing professionals remember how our responsibilities extend beyond making the sale. This is true even when the purchases produce placebo effects, as in the beauty-and-beer study.

As long as you keep in mind your ethical obligations, use opportunities to prime the shopper. Here's one example I have in mind: You realize that when your shopper asks where an item's located, it's better to walk the shopper there than to extend your finger and say, "That way." You and your staff know the store layout so well that it's too easy to assume the shopper won't get lost on the way, even in a small store. Older shoppers are especially likely to feel offended by the extended finger—middle one or otherwise. Offended shoppers usually abandon their shopping carts and leave in frustration.

On the other hand, there are many shoppers—more often men than women—who prefer to walk around a store by themselves, and there are times—such as when there are few staff and many shoppers—when it's difficult to lead one customer to a destination. In these situations, we'd still like to encourage the shopper to travel. As the shopper walks, they've the opportunity to see more of your merchandise which might interest them and read more signage about the services you provide.

Researchers at New York University-Stern, University of Pittsburgh, and Drexel University[62] found that a coupon requiring shoppers to travel farther from their planned path to obtain the discounted item resulted in an average increase in spending of about $21. When the coupon didn't require wandering from the planned path, the increase was instead about $14. The researchers suggest that retailers use mobile technologies to identify a shopper's location in the store and offer a deal that requires travel to another part of the store along with navigation instructions.

A personal escort can be even better, though. As you walk with the customer, talk about the items you're passing by. You've heard what item the shopper is looking for, and you can see which items the shopper's already selected. What else might this shopper also benefit from having, but perhaps overlook? The firmly motivated shopper suffers from tunnel vision. They're on a targeted search. Subtly prime by being a guide with pride.

Telling your customer a brief story as you stroll helps deliver the lesson. When the story contains a bit of a mystery, this can be especially effective. That's because solving the little mystery involves the customer's brain with what you're saying.

Right now, you're my customer who's interested in learning more about increasing your retailing profitability. So I'll tell you a story which involves not one, but two mysteries. The first mystery is this: I sharpened your wits earlier in this chapter with the primes of "parachute" and "bagpipe," Now I'll ask you what type of event is being described by the following brief story.

> They couldn't decide exactly what to play. Jerry eventually took a stand and set things up. Karen's recorder filled the room with soft and pleasant music. Finally, Mike said, "Let's hear the score." They listened carefully and commented on their performance.

Have you made your decision about what sort of event these people are commenting on? That solves the first mystery, so I'll tell you about a study conducted by education researcher Richard C. Anderson and his colleagues at University of Illinois-Urbana-Champaign:[63] Thirty students with a music education major and thirty students with a physical education major read a longer version of the story I just told you and were then assessed regarding what they thought the story described.

The music education students tended to believe the story described a rehearsal session of a woodwind ensemble. The P.E. students were more likely to say this was a description of playing card games.

Please read the brief story again now to verify how it could be interpreted in more than one way. It's pretty easy to see. However, in the University of Illinois research study, the participants who interpreted the story in one way gave no evidence that they could have interpreted it differently.

Oh, remember I said there were two mysteries here? The second one: Why am I telling you about this research study? The answer: To make the point that to help improve your profitability, you and your staff should stay tuned into what the shopper already knows. The words and terms they're familiar with. The way the shopper defines those words. The emotions those words appear to arouse in the shopper.

It's another of the tools to sell well.

Hey, that's a rhyme!

RIMinders

- Subtly mimic the behavior of your shopper. Listen carefully not only to the words the shopper is using, but also to their tone of voice. Watch the shopper's gestures and facial expressions.
- Attract shoppers by offering a never-ending panoply of new experiences. But always temper the change with comfortable repetition. Enable shoppers to revisit the already done.
- If you don't carry the best-known brand in your store, high-similarity copycats can sell well. On the other hand, if you stock the best-known brand adjacent to the copycats, you'll do best carrying moderate-similarity copycats.
- In general, use with shoppers measurement units familiar to them for that category of item. Beyond this general rule, if you want to leave with the shopper the impression of higher magnitude, such as the length of a warranty, then quote in smaller units, such as "84 months" instead of "seven years." But if you want to make things seem smaller, as with treatment duration, quote in larger units, such as "three weeks" instead of "twenty-one days."
- Repeat the benefits of a product to a shopper three times in different ways and the shopper is more likely to be convinced what you are saying is true. Effective repetition can be in the sound of the words. Rhythmic rhyming enhances perceptions of truth.
- Analyze ways in which placing products adjacent to each other on shelves affects sales.

- Smile often. Your smile boosts motivation to buy even among those who don't see you smile, but are around others who have seen you smile.
- Use discount coupons which require the shopper to travel to different parts of your store and distribute those coupons early in the shopping sequence.
- As you guide each shopper to the location of a product they asked about, tell brief stories about the items you're passing by.

6

Stimulation

~

In what may go down in retailing history as the ultimate "come as you are" shopping event, Priss, a grocery store close to the German-Danish border, celebrated its grand opening by offering a €270 shopping spree to the first 100 consumers who traversed the aisles completely in the nude. To the surprise of the store manager, there were about 250 takers, some of whom had camped out overnight. To curb the bedlam, which seemed to include even more photographers than naked shoppers, police monitors were recruited.

I'm thinking that the presence of those photographers and police grew the hype for Priss exponentially. I'm also suspecting some of those bare-bottomed buyers were enjoying the exposure as much as getting the free groceries.

Maybe you'll not want to include strip-downs in your special events. Instead, you could have people wear a costume. Consider the benefits:

- **The silly look.** If your wardrobe requirements are outlandish, you'll draw the sort of media attention we call publicity. The costumed shoppers can hear about and see their pictures online afterwards.

- **The naughtiness.** Some retailers give incentives to shoppers for dressing in pajamas. People associate wearing pajamas with relaxing their inhibitions. Actually, almost any costume can work. Think about adult Halloween parties! And when consumers relax their inhibitions in your store, they buy more.

- **The celebration.** E-commerce retailers could have fans post photos or videos of themselves in costume in order to earn a price discount. Those are fine techniques. Still, it's certainly more fun to wear your crazy costume to a store where you can bask in the reactions of others to you and express your reactions to the others there.

Publicity, naughtiness, celebration. These stimulate shoppers.

Another example of shopper stimulation is the flash mob. Want to transform passersby into fans of your store? Have a flash mob serenade them. Use songs to blow them away—and toward your shelves and racks.

A flash mob is a group of people who assemble suddenly in a public place, perform an unusual and sometimes seemingly pointless act for a brief time, then disperse. Song performances in food courts and mass dancing in train stations are flash mob events many have seen on internet videos.

When flash mobbing began, the objective was to surprise the merchants and shoppers. Not long afterwards, some centers began planning the intrusions. There were two reasons for this. First, retailers recognized that the performances can bring excitement to the shopping experience and online social media publicity afterwards. Second, retailers wanted to avoid the evil form of the flash mob—what I call a "smash mob"—in which unwary staff go mentally numb and close down their sensory channels while the mob steals merchandise. Breaking into song shouldn't lead to breaking into the store.

Researchers at Simon Fraser University[64] examined the effects on consumers in a public market of having a prearranged flash mob surprise shoppers by singing opera. The study compared what happened with the music presented live, the music presented from a recording, and no music.

As expected, the live music produced more consumer arousal and more positive feelings about the shopping experience than did the other two conditions. Both these increase the potential for purchases.

Beyond this, the flash mobs resulted in more feelings of connectedness to the shopping environment and more consumer-to-consumer interaction.

The music led to people forming groups temporarily because of enjoyment of the music and the experience. This phenomenon, too, can increase shopping basket dollar averages.

When people purchase in groups, each shopper's cart tends to ring up a higher total than if those same people had shopped alone. They are more likely to make what we think of as impulse purchases. A major reason this happens is that consumers in groups become more willing to take on risks, and it is the fear of risks behind resistances to buying.

Participants in the Simon Fraser University study responded positively to the opera music overall. Certainly, plenty of other people would prefer other styles of music. The magic of the flash mob is in the surprise and the live presence. These can come with a wide range of serenade motifs.

You'll benefit from using a wide range over time because what stimulates shoppers can become downright boring with repetition. These days, flash mobs are rather passé. You might consider stimulating with more extreme experiences.

One evening at Brooklyn Kitchen in New York City, the server announced, "And for the next item in tonight's Mexican feast, may I offer you a smoked corn custard sprinkled with pale yellow, squirming wax moth larvae?"

This isn't your cup of tea—or your cup of chapulines, those little fried grasshoppers which could be described as tasting like the exoskeleton of a potato chip? Still, remember the dangers of marketing to the mirror. Your shoppers may rush toward what you'd rush away from. Exotic experiences usually draw interest in, and therefore footsteps to, your retail business. Whether you run a restaurant, a museum, a travel agency, or some other type of business altogether, think of what unusual experiences you might offer to your target audiences.

Then, as you plan the publicity for these events, consider what benefits the unusual experiences provide:

- **Roller Coaster Effect.** Consumers go on the most treacherous roller coasters not only for the stimulating physical sensations, but also for the sense of pride achieved in prevailing over fears. To draw shoppers, publicize the thrill of confronting the exotic. Tell people they'll be able to take away a memento to verify their show of courage.

- **Exotic Dancer Effect.** Some people are more interested in breaking taboos than in breaking through fears. We don't call those ladies "exotic dancers" because they hail from faraway places. As a general rule, consumers yearn to push the limits. Publicize the opportunities you're giving people to do that.

- **Educational Effect.** The organizers of the Brooklyn Kitchen event touted the benefits from learning about cultures in which eating bugs is common. The Travel Channel regularly introduced viewers to exotic places with presentations of Andrew Zimmern's "Bizarre Foods" international ingestion interludes. Publicize how the extreme experiences you're offering will tickle the intellect.

Revise the merchandise mix and the merchandise arrangement in your store regularly so that you're offering your repeat customers endless new stimulation. People will go back to see that movie, read that book, or visit that vacation location they really enjoyed, but the more times they repeat the same experience, the less likely they are to do it again.

Announce the changes you've made in your store. If you've a fair amount of walk-in traffic, modify display windows and other areas shoppers will see as they stroll by. In ads, show images of the areas you've changed.

Then point out the changes to customers while they are shopping.

In conversations with your shoppers about what's in your store, telescope time for them: Remind them of the variety of experiences they've had when shopping in your store. We often forget all of the variety we've actually had in our lives and instead focus on how repetitive our experiences have been. By reminding the customer of prior buying trips—or asking the customer if there have been prior buying trips—we generate a sense of variety.

If the actual range of alternatives in your store is relatively small, you'll portray the assortment as larger if you organize the display by a dimension of interest to the shopper, but not of primary interest. Organize by price, for example. It takes time for the shopper to run their eyes over whatever is there. The increased time translates in the shopper's mind to the impression of a larger item assortment.

If the actual variety is large, organize your display by a dimension of primary interest to the shopper. Take the case of shoppers who are familiar with the product category. For luxury products, their organizing rubric might be brand name. The consumer's eyes home in on their favorite brand. For high-technology items, where the latest versions carry more features or more status, the shopper's organizing principle, and therefore your rule for organizing the items in your store, might be release date or the operating system generation.

Now let's take the case of the shopper who has limited familiarity with the product category. They're purchasing the item such as a carbon monoxide detector or a patterned scarf because someone told them they really need one. How should you portray that you do, in fact, have a large assortment? Here, organize your selection by circumstances of use. For the CO detector, it might be residential versus commercial. For the scarves, it might be formal versus informal wardrobe.

Consumers overestimate the amount of variety they want. Carnegie Mellon University[65] students were offered a bonus treat in their economics or history class: They could select snacks to be given to them at the end of three successive class sessions. The choices included Snickers bars, Oreo cookies, milk chocolate with almonds, tortilla chips, peanuts, and cheese-peanut butter crackers.

Since the offer was part of a consumer behavior study, though, the sponsors had to make sure the choice process wasn't all that simple. For half the number of classes, the students were invited to choose one item on each of the three weeks. At each session, they weren't told if there would be additional opportunities to choose in future classes. The students in the other classes in the study were told that in the first class session, they were to select the treat they wanted for each of three classes in advance.

Among the students who selected all three treats in advance, 45% of the participants chose three different items. In the other group, only 8% of the participants ended up choosing three different items. If members of this group picked the Snickers bar as their treat for the first class session, they pretty much stuck with the Snickers bar for the next two sessions.

People overestimate the extent to which they'll get tired of consuming the same item. They think they'll want to make a change when, in fact, they'll end up continuing to pick the familiar favorite. When offered a range of alternatives, people see it as an opportunity to try out something new. Some people find it easier to say, "Give me one of each," than to carefully assess the tradeoffs in the choices.

Many shoppers are tempted to switch what they buy for no reason other than that they think they'll enjoy the variety. If you want to introduce the customer to a new brand, their interest in switching is fine. However, if the brand the customer has been buying delivers good value for them and high profits for you, I'd think you'd prefer to at least delay the brand switching, short of completely eliminating it.

Again, we can slow down switching by encouraging the variety-seeking customer to think about other alternatives they've already tried. If the shopper talks about purchasing a different brand "to break out of my routine," ask, "What are some other brands you've used in the past, and what convinced you to start using our brand you're using now?"

If the customer is talking about holding off on a purchase so they can try out a store that opened recently in the area, ask, "What are some of the stores you've shopped at before or in addition to shopping here, and what about our store keeps you coming back?"

Most people rise to the challenge when asked a question. They might not answer aloud, but you've probably started them thinking.

It is not a matter of the more reasons, the better, though. If you ask the consumer to generate loads of reasons to buy the particular product or to shop at your store, the task becomes more difficult for the customer, and this actually makes your preferred alternative less attractive.

This tactic is an example of how what we do might make us money for a combination of reasons. The customer's answers to these questions not only provide "virtual variety," but also give us the chance to find out what's important to this individual shopper and then use this information to make our case for the shopper forgetting about switching. Instead, we'll work to show the customer different ways to use the same items they've been using up to now. Even a change in the circumstances under which your product is used could add enough variety to prolong shopper interest.

When you introduce a new product line in your store, you hope to increase total sales. If profits from the new line do no more than equal profits from the existing lines, that hope hasn't been fulfilled. Worse yet is if revenues from one segment eat up revenues from other segments.

What are the best ways to turn cannibalization to your advantage?

Researchers at University of Virginia[66] tracked results when a specialty apparel retailer installed a store-within-a-store (SWAS) boutique which featured a new label. Installation of the SWAS improved three metrics for the overall store—the percentage of shoppers converted into purchasers, the dollar amount of the average customer transaction in the store, and growth in sales. It appears that a SWAS is a good idea.

When consumers feel there's a natural fit between the SWAS item lines and the other item lines, this increases customer spending on both sets. One explanation is the added excitement from introducing the new product lines. There are other ways to add to your store the sort of excitement which will draw shopper interest. The SWAS is only one alternative. But it does appear the SWAS way has a lasting influence. If you choose this alternative for building profits, expect more in sales climbs of the existing lines than in sales climbs of the added lines. To refresh the excitement periodically, you might decide to use the SWAS space for different lines over time. When retailers have a part of the store set aside for seasonal items, they are using a variant of this technique.

If the consumer perceives a very high fit between the two sets of product lines, sales on the SWAS lines will drop over time, while sales on the older lines will end up increasing. The reason seems to be that shoppers try out the variety of the new lines, but conclude they're getting equivalent products with the two lines, and they prefer the reliability of the older lines. Perhaps this is because the older lines are a time-tested alternative and/or the price of the older lines is lower. In your store, it would make the most sense to introduce a SWAS only if there is some distinction from the existing lines.

Stimulation must be bold enough to make a difference in the consumer's brain. You want your selling messages to be prominent so they'll catch the attention of shoppers. The payoff is convincing the prospect to make the purchase. But you have to catch the attention first. And yes, there are ways to draw in the consumer aside from message prominence. Still, your attention to perception is fundamental.

- **Live large.** Consumers are more likely to notice bigger ads than smaller ones and to listen more closely to the same salesperson when she's making effusive gestures rather than restrained movements. Enthusiasm persuades, particularly when the enthusiasm is genuine.

- **Color consumers' worlds.** Signage which employs a range of hues grabs more attention than the black-and-white. It is also true that B&W commands attention when surrounded by colorful stimuli, but this effect is weaker.

- **Be bold.** Product claims made in boldface print or in a slow, deep voice achieve perceptual prominence. Women find special appeal in a creaky male voice.[67] To turn shoppers' heads, surprise them with daring humor or unexpected claims. Do be sure to promptly follow up with a comforting resolution, though.

- **Cement with concrete.** Concrete words like apple, engine, and hammer are easier for consumers to process than abstract words like aptitude, essence, and hatred. Because they are easier to process, these words will stand out. This is not to say you should completely avoid abstract words. Once you stop the shopper with the prominent stimuli, you'd like them to spend time contemplating what you're saying. Abstract words help do that.

The shopper psychology underpinning for all of this is Weber's Law: In the 1830's, Ernst Weber reported that weight lifters would notice an increase or decrease in the load only when the change was about 20% of the prior load. For 100 pounds, it took a 20 pound difference. But for 300 pounds, it took a 60 pound difference. Experimental psychologist Gustav Theodor Fechner extended Weber's Law to cover all sorts of human perceptions, including whatever the shopper in your store encounters.

To achieve prominence, make the ads, gestures, signage, wording, and the rest about 20% different from what surrounds it. If everything in your communication comes across to the consumer as really loud, the loud won't stand out. In addition, odds are with you ending up annoying the person.

An underappreciated resource to add stimulation to a store is clutter. From late 2009 through early 2011, many Big Box retailers tidied up aisles and shelves. They wanted to carry less inventory in economically uncertain times. Then there was miniaturization and digitizing. When you're selling pocket toys instead of those of traditional build and music phones instead of CD players, there's less need to cram in the merchandise.

In some cases, the cleanup came from a realization that consumers were wanting to keep all things more straightforward in their lives, again because of the economically uncertain times. Loblaw Companies Limited—Canada's largest grocery retailer—rolled out their "Clutter-Free Check Out Lanes," and Superquinn in Ireland moved in that same direction.

Walmart cut down on the clutter in order to attract shoppers from Target. End caps got narrower, the floor-toward-ceiling power aisle shelves got much shorter, and people coming from opposite directions could actually navigate two shopping carts comfortably past each other.

That was then. Walmart shoppers loved the spaciousness. Customer satisfaction surged. On the other hand, the size of the average sale plummeted. In response, Walmart ultimately went back to plumping up the racks and cluttering up the aisles. The motto seems to have become, "If they trip over it, they might decide to buy it."

There's something else at work, too: Research says clutter implies low prices. And this is where you can make a strategic decision. You could go for the clutter to play to the increased price sensitivity of consumers. Or you could distinguish yourself and have the opportunity to set higher prices by holding out for neatness.

Don't overdo it, though. Consumers need sufficient complexity to stay engaged. In Chapter 2, I described how making the potato chip bag harder to open increased the value placed on the item. A classic and repeated finding in consumer psychology is that we want to introduce enough incongruity, enough surprise, so that the shopper slows down for a moment to appreciate the sales message. If the layout is overly sterile, the viewer processes it all immediately and then moves on—beyond the range of a possible add-on or upgrade which would benefit both the shopper and the retailer.

Introducing a new alternative to the consumer? Then present a mystery. This is a technique to be used with caution. In Chapter 5, we saw how mysterious disappearances of words like "parachute" and "bagpipe" could frustrate a shopper. But when done well, a mystery ad can be surprisingly effective. Notably, magnetizing with mystery arouses the consumer's interest in a small to midsize retail business that wants to distinguish itself from larger competitors.

Also consider how this can profit you with an unfamiliar alternative carrying ambiguous category designations:

Let's say that in a product line you already carry, you're offering a new brand which has unusual features—such as a dog food sold frozen. The prospective purchaser may be uncertain what category it belongs to—in this case, either the pet food category or the frozen food category.

Or you're introducing a multifunction product—such as an exercise device and MP3 player—where it could be placed in different categories—in this case, either the exercise device category or the music player category.

Or you're a new store in town, and with the objective of succeeding through diversification, you offer an assortment of products crossing traditional category designations—such as carrying sporting goods, camping supplies, and house paint.

The challenge is to position the new offering in the consumer's mind so they know what category or categories to place it into. You see, people are more comfortable shopping when they know the category.

One advertising alternative is to announce the brand, item, or store name and then boldly tell the consumer what category you want them to place it into. In doing this, you're counting on the audience caring. Often, they don't.

The "mystery ad" alternative consists of waiting until the end of the ad to announce the name. Start off with an unusual story or absurd humor that dramatizes the category—exercise machine, let's say—but hooks the ad's viewer or listener into thinking, "What's this commercial for, anyway?"

Mystery ads are significantly more effective than traditional ads in making the name-category link memorable via stimulation of the viewer's curiosity. Don't sustain the mystery for too long, though. Be sure to announce the name at the end boldly. Advertising pioneer David Ogilvy said long ago, "Use the name within the first ten seconds." Mystery ads change that advice to, "Drill in the name within the last five seconds."

Another source of stimulation—the color of a product—strongly affects its attractiveness to consumers. The color of an orange juice is more of an influence on how taste is perceived than is information about the price of the juice or claims about its quality. And shoppers searching for the right shirt, interior paint, or nail polish pay lots of attention to hue.

What about the names given to colors? Is a retailer better off carrying products labeled "cherry red" rather than just "red" on the package? Is a car salesman or interior designer likely to make better sales saying "passion blue" instead of "medium blue," even though the automobile or the carpet swatch is right there for the customer to see for themselves?

It turns out that Shakespeare's Juliet may have had her accuracy clouded by love when she uttered, "What's in a name? that which we call a rose By any other name would smell as sweet."

Unexpected color names—like "Florida orange" and "freckle brown" build interest. Color names which venture beyond surprise to blatant ambiguity—names like "antique red" and "millennium orange"—can be better still. Ambiguous names work best when the shopper doesn't see the actual product color first, while unexpected descriptive names work best when the product color is seen. The reason for all this is that the shopper spends mental energy trying to figure out why the particular color name was used. As we've already seen, mental involvement increases purchase likelihood.

However, note that high stimulation of the wrong sort will fatigue your shopper. In a classic Case Western University[68] study in which the stimulation consisted of resisting temptation, participants had been asked to skip a meal before arriving at the site, so they were no doubt hungry. Welcoming the participants was the aroma of freshly-baked chocolate chip cookies. Then each participant was assigned to sit in front of an individual table for five minutes.

For one group of participants, the table contained no food. For a second group, the table contained cookies, chocolates, and radishes. These participants were invited to eat whatever they wanted. Participants in the third group also had the cookies, chocolates, and radishes on the table, and they, too, were invited to eat. But to eat only the radishes. This limitation was revealed to the unlucky participants in the third group with the explanation, "You have been assigned to the radish condition."

After the five minutes, each participant embarked on a difficult task, paralleling the sort of decision making involved in a highly complicated purchase. What the researchers measured was how long each participant was willing to stay at the task. What they found was that the radish people gave up much more quickly than did the cookie people or the no-food people.

Retailers should give shoppers a brief break from challenging purchase choices. The outcome is likely to be an increase in sales.

Breaks also increase enjoyment. It's an example of what psychologists call habituation. Consider the massage therapy category of services retailing. Massage therapists report that the client generally likes the massage more when they're rubbed for a while, pounded for a while, kneaded for a while, and then rubbed again than if there's no change.

A provocative consumer research finding was reported in an article titled, "Enhancing the Television Viewing Experience through Commercial Interruptions."[69] People gave higher average ratings of TV programs when the programs included advertising breaks than when the programs didn't.

Skeptical?

Some consumer behavior researchers' conclusions won't make sense to you because they are, in fact, erroneous. But before dismissing these findings about commercial breaks improving viewer enjoyment, ask yourself if you might have overlooked factors the researchers discovered.

People are often bad at predicting their behavior when asked directly. Consumers say they'd enjoy programs more without ads. They pay for devices to eliminate ads and to see commercial-free programming. But this does not, in itself, mean that those people would rate programming with commercials as less enjoyable.

Anyway, since you're a retailer, you're probably more interested in how much people liked the commercials than in how much they liked the TV programs. It's the commercials that do the selling for you. How would liking the programming help bring in the money?

In the research studies, it turned out that those consumers exposed to the ads were willing to pay about 30% more for a DVD compilation of programs by the same director. Participants who watched a nature documentary with commercial breaks were willing to donate more to a nature charity after viewing. The enjoyment of the programming did translate into greater financial returns.

If you're producing infomercials, deliver the pitch in brief segments with changeups. The in-store version of the infomercial follows the same rules. When you do all the talking nonstop, you'll lose the prospect's attention.

Habituation is related to age. Commercial breaks improved the enjoyment more for younger than for older viewers. Changeups improve the enjoyment more for younger than for older consumers.

Innovative consumers have a special yearning for changeups. These consumers are of special value to retailers because of their openness to new product and service offerings, and innovative consumers are stimulated by playfulness. When you sell products which attract state-of-the-art or creative thinking, accommodate people who want to play around with the items and want to be playful with store staff.

Playful activities are spontaneous, inventive, and changeable. Retailers aiming to provide for playfulness will want to regularly introduce novel products and rotate assignments in ways which allow for changing interactions with staff.

Still, even innovative shoppers may hold back on the opportunities to be playful until they become somewhat familiar with the merchandise and the store. The familiarity motivation discussed in the prior chapter rarely fades completely. Don't assume that an early hesitation indicates a lack of interest in playfulness later.

Some retailers and researchers have said that showering a shopper with a variety of items all at once will encourage the sort of playfulness which increases the probability of making a sale. However, because facing more items means taking more time to gain familiarity with each, this showering suggestion doesn't wash.

Further, giving the innovative consumer opportunities to play doesn't assure a sale. Due to the flexible thinking of the innovator, the play might satisfy, on its own, whatever was motivating the purchase.

For instance, there's the stick. In year 2008, the stick was inducted into the National Toy Hall of Fame, headquartered in Rochester, New York. Thus, the stick joined the likes of Tonka Trucks, Mr. Potato Head, and Barbie, each one an inductee from an earlier year.

A plain stick. Not a pogo stick, a hockey stick, or a pool stick. Each of those others could be considered a plaything to purchase. Yet, as the National Toy Hall of Fame induction announcement makes clear, the plain stick could fill in. For an innovative consumer, the stick becomes a sword, a baton, a big league slugger's baseball bat, or some other variety of magic wand. In the hands of the playful artist, sticks are a foundation for collages, sculptures, and structures.

This seems to me evidence that even for the most mundane of items for sale, you can stimulate with a game. Customers have always loved to play games used as sales promotions. Scratch-off discounts. Sweepstakes. "Design our new logo" or "Name our new service" or "Tell us in 25 words or less why you shop at our store."

In the early days, retailers believed there needed to be real, tangible prizes for maximum participant involvement, although the value of the prizes often could be quite modest. People got involved for the joy of the contest. More recently, marketers are finding that no extrinsic reward at all is needed if the excitement of the game is sufficient.

The most engaging online games have a storyline. Stories stimulate. Products sell better when each item comes with a tale to give it distinction. Vendors of antiques, art objects, and handmade crafts find that easier to do than those who sell toasters or toilet paper. With the toasters, toilet paper, and other commodity items, the background narrative sometimes should best be about the store itself.

A backstory could be told online and in a paper catalog. In whatever way a compelling backstory is delivered, the entertainment prolongs the shopper's attention, giving you the opportunity to dramatize the benefits the consumer would find in purchasing the product. Backstories also give your customers conversation starters as they generate word-of-mouth about your store and the offerings.

Have product literature available to your shoppers to take away with them not just before they complete the purchase, but also afterwards. Invite them to come back to inform you how the purchase worked out, and when they come back with a happy tale, admire their skills in making the right decision. Then use snippets from those tales to build the backstory further when talking to the next round of shoppers.

A backstory delivered face-to-face to the customer adds the appeal of exclusivity. The impression, deserved or not, is that the shopper is privileged to be told the tale.

Want to convince me to purchase an appliance maintenance contract from you? Stimulate me with stories.

A set of researchers at Ohio State University[70] wanted to compare the effectiveness of narratives and statistics in influencing consumers' opinions. In one study, they asked participants to estimate how likely it is that a refrigerator they might purchase would break down at some point. Before stating the estimate, each participant was told they'd be given information to assist them with the task. For one group, the information consisted of stories written by consumers about the times they'd had to deal with a refrigerator breaking down. Participants in the other group were given actual statistics about the frequency of appliance breakdowns.

Frequency estimates from those given the stories averaged about one-third higher than did the estimates from those given the statistics. The stories of trouble led the consumers to exaggerate the actual frequency of trouble. Narratives are more influential—and more memorable—than numbers.

What augments the power of a story?

- **Authenticity.** Make the story believable. Keep the important details the same each time you tell the story. Reports of outrageous outcomes in bizarre circumstances aren't influential.
- **Conciseness.** Keep it short. Make the point of each story crystal clear.
- **Humor.** This heads off mental counterarguments. The shopper is too busy chuckling to challenge the thrust of your story.
- **Reversal.** Use contrast in your story. Good versus evil. Natural versus artificial.

A story with a couple of twists is using the tool of reversal in order to stimulate the shopper. My tale to illustrate that point begins with the abundance of research documenting the power of a story in persuading shoppers to take a retailer's recommendation. Among these findings is a report from University of St. Gallen[71] in Switzerland. These researchers found how, as a general rule, it's better to say, "May I tell you a true story to show the advantages of this product?," than to say, "May I list for you the advantages of this product?"

Then comes the first twist to the University of St. Gallen tale: If the shopper senses that the retailer is being manipulative, the advantages of telling the story disappear. That happens even if the customer's suspiciousness didn't arise because of the retailer telling the true story.

Then, as in any fine tale, there is still another twist from the University of St. Gallen research results. It's something that might actually be considered a surprise ending: Even if the consumer senses the retailer is being manipulative, there is a way for the retailer to restore the persuasive advantages of the story. It is to fill the story with as much detail as the shopper's attention span seems to allow.

Therefore, you might want to say, "May I tell you a true story with all the details that show the advantages of this product?"

RIMinders

- Conduct special events for which shoppers are invited to wear costumes.
- Entertain shoppers, such as with unannounced musical performances or exotic food and beverage servings.
- Encourage your shoppers to come with groups of family and friends.
- Change the merchandise mix and the merchandise arrangement in your store regularly, and then announce the changes widely.
- If you want to slow a shopper's variety-seeking behavior, such as brand switching, remind the shopper of prior buying trips and ask questions like, "What are some other brands you've used in the past, and what convinced you to use our brand you're using now?" If the customer is talking about holding off on a purchase so they can try out a store that opened recently in the area, ask, "What are some of the stores you've shopped at before or in addition to shopping here, and what about our store keeps you coming back?"
- If the actual range of alternatives in your store is relatively small, portray the assortment as larger by organizing the display using a dimension of interest to the shopper, but not of primary interest.
- When consumers feel there's a natural fit between new item lines and existing item lines, but the two lines can be differentiated, this builds customer spending on both sets.

- If you want a message to make a difference in the consumer's brain, make it about 20% different from the surroundings and check that the message has sufficient complexity to be interesting.
- When introducing a product or business concept shoppers might find hard to classify, stimulate the shopper's curiosity, such as with ads that don't announce the product or concept name until the end.
- Give shoppers brief breaks during challenging purchase choices.
- Fill your true stories to your shopper with as much detail as the shopper's attention span seems to allow.

7

Trust

Want to swindle your shoppers? Then learn from the business model of the Nigerian 419 Scam, as described in a 2012 Microsoft Research paper titled "Why Do Nigerian Scammers Say They Are from Nigeria?" The Nigeria 419 Scam is the one where the target of the swindle gets an e-mail saying that if the target sends money or their bank account information, they'll end up receiving an incredibly large amount in return. It's called the Nigerian 419 Scam because the e-mail solicitation comes from Nigeria and the section in the Nigerian criminal code forbidding the scam is numbered 419.

But, of course, you don't want to swindle shoppers. In this case, there's still something to be learned from the Microsoft Research paper. The answer to the question "Why Do Nigerian Scammers Say They Are from Nigeria?" is that the scammers want to qualify their prospects quickly. Figuring that many people already know about the Nigerian Scam, an e-mail coming from Nigeria with improbable tales of West African riches and a request for the recipient to send their own riches will quickly eliminate all but the gullible.

It's the gullible the perpetrators of the swindle are aiming to entice. A Nigerian Scam sufficiently profitable for the swindlers requires a substantial amount of back-and-forth coaxing. The maximum return comes from continuing to milk the cash cow. Only the highly trusting will stay with it long enough.

Because the gullible consumers' guard is down, their trust in the Nigerian 419 Scam is misplaced. Because most of your shoppers' guardedness is way up due to knowledge of scams like the Nigerian 419, you'll want to work to legitimately earn and maintain the trust of your shoppers. By doing so, you'll mobilize a distinctive tool to sell well.

How fair do your shoppers consider the world to be? To what degree do they think the people they know generally get what those people deserve?

The answers to those questions influence how much trust your shoppers place in the recommendations you make to them. Moreover, although you've only limited influence over your shoppers' perceptions of fairness in life, you have enough influence to produce a difference in buying intentions.

But the effect sets in after, not before, the consumer makes the purchase decision. Researchers at Saint Mary's College of California and Canada's York University[72] surveyed perceptions of life fairness among about 500 study participants. Along with this, the participants were asked to choose between two digital cameras, both of which had been recommended by the salesperson.

Prior to the choice, the consumer's degree of trust in the recommendations had little to do with life fairness beliefs. However, after having made the choice, those with high life fairness beliefs were more likely than those without to say they trusted the salesperson's recommendations.

Also, in accord with the story I used to end the prior chapter, if the consumers believe the salesperson is intentionally misleading them, the life-fairness effect on trust disappears altogether. And the effect is much stronger when consumers are considering purchases they're making for themselves rather than for others.

Putting it all together: If you can convince your customers that life is fair, they're more likely to trust your recommendations for a series of decisions they make in purchases of items for their own use.

As to how to increase belief in life fairness, establish a record of keeping your promises. Then to grow trust most efficiently, persuade the consumer to behave in a trusting way. Not only keep your promises to your customers, but also point out to the customers that the promises have been kept and there have been benefits from this.

An example is with MBGs. A common practice in retailing is to accept products back for a full refund, even if the product has been partially used. The retailer might insist on issuing a store credit for a future purchase rather than making a cash refund. But sophisticated retailers know a customer is more likely to make purchases at a store offering the promise of money-back guarantees—MBGs.

The MBG affects both the shoppers' logic and their emotions. At the logical level, it is insurance, letting shoppers know that if anything goes wrong, the cost to make things right will be limited to getting the remnants of the merchandise back to you. "Just bring the item in for a full refund."

At the emotional level, the influence of the MBG is assurance. When you, the retailer, offer your customer an MBG, you're encouraging the customer to have high trust the product will deliver on what's been promised. This second prong—the emotional—is more influential than the logical.

Because of the power of the MBG, feature this policy in your marketing. Emphasize the assurance you're offering, with the insurance angle as a subtheme. Puff up the trust.

An MBG is a multi-part agreement with your customers:
- What you are promising you will do
- The rules for deciding if you've kept that promise
- The remedies available to the customer if you fail to keep your promise
There's a fourth part as well:
- How you will answer the customer's questions about each of the first three parts. The MBG is one tool for projecting your marketing identity to your target customers. Use your explanation of the guarantee to project clearly.

Stay aware of the emotional prong as you analyze what you're promising. Keep both the commitments and the explanations up-to-date.

When considering the wisdom of MBGs in your business model, your thoughts may quickly drift to the topic of serial returners. These are the nuisance consumers who use items and then come back to the store asking for a full refund. When you set the rules for MBG returns and give explanations to the serial returners, you may want to keep them as customers. If so, show respect, concern, and empathy while protecting your business from exploitation, even unintentional exploitation.

Not that most shoppers are out to exploit you. On the contrary, when a large remedy—such as reimbursement for the entire purchase price—is made for what was a minor inconvenience—such as a vending machine taking a long time to respond—the consumer feels uncomfortable. If a bank offered to match with bank funds the amount of a slow ATM withdrawal, the bank customer would start to doubt the fiduciary skills of the place they've trusted with their savings.

Although bragging that you offer a "money-back guarantee" builds trust, talk of an "unconditional guarantee" does not to the same extent. Consumers are less likely to believe an unconditional guarantee than an attribute-specific guarantee, which lists the circumstances under which the retailer will take remedial action.

Certain other well-intentioned phrases eat away at trust: "I can give you a free estimate with no obligation on your part." Consumers expect there to be no charge for an estimate, so "free estimate" comes across as bragging about nothing. The consumer then questions the value of real benefits you describe afterwards. Shoppers become more likely to purchase out of obligation after getting an estimate. The problem is that if you say, "with no obligation on your part," you reduce the obligation the prospect feels. Avoid the problems by using, "May I run the numbers?"

Another example of phrasing that eats away at trust: Say to me during the sales pitch, "I'll be honest with you," and I'll respond inside my head, "What? Were you lying to me up to now?"

Yet, researchers at University of Minnesota, Utrecht University, and University of Twente[73] found, across six laboratory and real-world telemarketing studies, brief chitchat at the start, such as "How are you today?" softens up the prospect's resistances to a solicitation which follows.

The components of familiarity I discussed in Chapter 5 interact with the determinants of trust. We're more likely to trust what's familiar to us, and we're more likely to accept the familiar when we trust the source. So I can give you an example, please allow me to return one last time to the topic of measurement units. Which would a consumer prefer—a GPS unit with battery power sufficient to last two hours or a more bulky, more expensive unit with battery power sufficient to last three hours? In the actual study,[74] only 26% of the consumers preferred the two-hour unit when those specifications were announced by the experimenter. Then an equivalent group of consumers were given the same information using different measurement units, more familiar for such comparisons—"up to 120 minutes" and "up to 180 minutes." Now the percentage preferring the two-hour unit more than doubled—to 57%.

Except not for everybody. The increase occurred only among those consumers who said they considered the experimenter to be a trustworthy source of product information. The more general point is that each of the components I'm describing to you in separate chapters for clarity does, in application, interact with the others.

Pictures, especially familiar pictures, build trust. My research example for this one has to do with the sale of beliefs more than with directly selling products, but I promise to end up bringing it back to the store:

Researchers at Victoria University of Wellington in New Zealand[75] presented study participants with declarative statements like, "Giraffes are the only mammals that cannot jump" and "Turtles are deaf." These statements were chosen because most people are unsure of their truth.

Those participants shown a photo of a giraffe along with the statement were more likely to say it was true than were the participants shown only the statement. Similarly, a photo of a turtle injected credibility into the "Turtles are deaf" statement.

This phenomenon is not limited to people who know little about a topic. When neurological conclusions were presented to brain scientists, those scientists also shown brain scan photos attributed more credibility, on average, to the neurological conclusions. Yet the photos used in the study were not at all objectively related to what was said to the brain scientists about the neurological conclusions.

In my opinion, an important factor in these studies was the use of photos rather than artistic illustrations. Photos come across as more realistic. Drawings might imply subjectivity, which would make the claim less believable. I do admit that the inclusion of brief text did result in the effect, though

Based on their findings, the researchers say that showing a photo of a smiling person holding a product you sell makes it more likely consumers viewing the photo would believe a claim such as, "This product is easy to use." So would a paragraph of text describing how the product was manufactured. Neither the photo nor the paragraph need to directly document ease of use.

A related shopper psychology pointer is that people anxious to complete a purchase will welcome evidence you give them that they're making a good decision, even if the evidence you provide is objectively irrelevant to the decision.

Is it okay to fool consumers, convincing them of the validity of a belief or a value of a product through illusion? There is an answer to this question having to do with ethics, but from a research-based perspective, one answer is that we may not be jeopardizing trust. The sense of well-being that comes from a mistaken perception is as strong as one coming from an accurate perception. It occurs at the level of brain physiology.

Please consider that when I use the term "brain physiology," I speak with authority, since it was during a summer break while I was an undergraduate at UCLA many decades ago that I first performed brain surgery.

I wasn't doing this solo. I worked under highly competent supervision. My surgery assignments were part of a neuropsychology honors program at the prestigious Brain Research Institute.

I also should tell you that I performed the surgery not on people, but on laboratory rats.

The purpose of the project was to explore what is called intracranial self-stimulation. I implanted small electrodes in pleasure centers of the brain. Then the rat could give itself a tiny electric pulse by pressing a bar.

This direct stimulation of pleasure centers altered behavior without the need for traditional rat payoffs like food. The electric pulse was so rewarding that the rat had to be disconnected from the apparatus periodically. Otherwise, the animal would press itself to the point of collapse, never taking time to drink, eat, or sleep. The principle of pleasure deriving from physiological well-being had been violated in our experiments.

Even if we don't want our customers to shop until they drop, let's stimulate the shopping pleasure centers. Since we won't be literally hard-wired into the human shopper's brain, like I'd done with the rats in the Brain Research Institute studies, pleasure is more strongly associated with what the consumer thinks they are experiencing than with what they are actually experiencing.

Researchers at Stanford University[76] asked people to taste five wines and to rate their quality. Unlike in the wine study I described in Chapter 2, these participants were told not the country of origin of the wine, but rather the price. There were five price points, which ranged from inexpensive to expensive. What the study participants did not know was that the five wines they were tasting actually came from only three different bottles. One pair was presented as two different wines, both at a $45 price point and at a $5 price point. This was also true for another pair of wines.

On brain scans, people tasting the $45 wines showed enhanced activity in an area of the brain associated with consumer decision making based on emotions. Compared to when a study participant tasted a wine identified as low-priced, the participant tasting the identical wine identified as high-priced experienced greater pleasure of the sort that translates into an increased likelihood of buying the wine.

So do you consider it okay to offer to shoppers illusions which bring them pleasure?

Before you answer, I'll ask another question: What is the retailer's responsibility when selling a remedy that works, but the retailer believes it is working only because the recipient expects it to?

- Parkinson's disease sufferers have reported less agitation after a regimen of a pill that contains no known bioactive ingredients.
- Saltwater injections often relieve pain nearly as well as does a morphine injection.
- Toothaches have been shown to be relieved by a procedure the patient is told is an ultrasound machine, but in fact is nothing more than official-looking equipment making noises.

This appears to be a placebo effect of the sort I noted in Chapter 5 when describing the beauty & beer study.

Is it legitimate to use such pills, injections, and procedures as part of medical care? After all, the saltwater and the sugar pill are likely to have fewer side effects than the morphine and L-dopa.

For me, the ethicality depends on relative risks, candor, and inquisition.

Yet another example of what seems to be a placebo effect is how knee pain can be relieved by a fake operation, in which the leg is opened and then closed, with nothing else done. Here, the potential risks from surgery are such that recommending a fake operation is, in my opinion, ethically wrong. Based on this logic, if there are less invasive methods for pain relief than a saltwater injection, those alternatives would be the legitimate choice.

A placebo effect works even when the consumer is told the mechanism of action is unknown. Only relatively recently[77] has evidence accumulated about precisely what verifiable neurophysiological changes cause mindful meditation to reduce high blood pressure and relieve depression. Still, up to now, it has seemed to me to be quite legitimate to say to patients, "Many people report positive results with mindful meditation, so I recommend you give it a try to discover the results for you." Similarly, it would be okay to say, "Many people have said they've achieved relief from Parkinson's agitation after using this pill. Medical researchers aren't certain exactly why it works. But because there have been no side effects reported, I recommend we try it as our first alternative."

Still to maintain consumer trust, a spirit of inquisitiveness is necessary for use of what we consider to be placebos. We need to press for explanations of how the pill or procedure is working. Maybe saltwater is diluting the toxins causing the pain. Maybe as we carefully assess mindful meditation, we'll see ways to simplify the routine without lessening the payoffs.

When closing a sale on mindful meditation or anything else, we might present a disclaimer to the consumer. With special sales promotions and contests, the disclaimer may have to do with exclusions. You can't use the coupon on weekends, or it isn't necessary to make a purchase in order to be a winner. For medications, the disclaimers may have to do with side effects and drug interactions. Because information processing takes mental energy, the pace at which we present the disclaimers affects how well the information leads to the trust we'd like to establish.

The conventional gospel is that you deliver any disclaimers at the end of the ad in order to emboss the main message first. The general practice is to use an announcer skilled in talking as quickly as possible, with the objective of the disclaimer not throwing interference into the ad's overall thrust.

These rapid-rate disclosures work well when your store has already built substantial trust among the audience for the ad. However, when you're establishing trust for your store brand, deliver disclaimers at the same pace the body of the ad is delivered, and in the same tone of voice from the same announcer. The rapid rate will come across as trying to pull a fast one—tricking the shopper by confusing them. The change in tempo leads to a decrease in purchase intentions.

With sales promotions and contests, always announce the restrictions with a measured tone. You don't want shoppers arriving at your store expecting to get a better deal than you promised to deliver. This would eat away at trust even for the store that's already established a deep reservoir. The negative feelings stimulated by this in shoppers are so strong that consumer psychologists refer to the package of emotions as "betrayal." Because it's so serious, also be sure the offer and disclaimers are in writing, and have each staff member carry a copy. It's better to have the customer and salesperson be both looking at a printed ad as their reference point when talking rather than resorting to memories of what the broadcast ad really said or engaging in a round of direct-gaze dueling eyeballs.

When the disclaimer's in writing, realize that the consumer probably won't read it all or adequately understand what it does say. In spring 2010, video game retailer GameStation added the following to their website's terms and conditions for placing an order:

> You agree to grant Us a nontransferable option to claim, for now and forevermore, Your immortal soul. Should We wish to exercise this option, You agree to surrender Your immortal soul, and any claim You may have on it, within 5 (five) working days of receiving written notification.

There was an opt-out checkbox. Yet, about 88% of the transactions were with acceptance of those terms and conditions during one day alone. In fact, it was only for that one day alone, since the day happened to be April 1. On the second of the month, with April Fools' Day having passed,

GameStation removed the immortal soul clause, plus announced that they were nullifying for now and forevermore the pledges collected.

Because few people will read the terms and conditions thoroughly when making a purchase decision, merchants can swindle, and even endanger, their customers. Disclosures of side effects on medicine bottles. Piles of documents presented for signature in order to forward a mortgage loan into escrow. Written notices of possible conflict of interest from attorneys, accountants, and financial advisors. Those doing the selling can too often figure that their ethical responsibility ends when they've buried the prospect in disclaimers.

It doesn't. Retailing ethics require giving to shoppers what they need to make an informed decision. To be sure, data overload corrupts informed decisions. It corrodes trust in retailing, which is destructive to all of us in the profession.

Be selective. Again, if you sense something is important for the customer to know, tell it to them. And if your intent is to mislead or betray, that's sinful. But presenting information selectively usually assists the consumer. Researchers at University of Twente in the Netherlands, University of Indiana, and University of Cincinnati[78] aimed to confuse study participants by adding to the sales pitch technical jargon, unfamiliar words, illogical product groupings, and dollar prices restated as cents. The result was that the participants chose items more quickly and with more certainty than would be in their best interests.

On the other hand, when a salesperson selectively volunteers negative information about a product that's being considered by the shopper, the shopper becomes more likely to trust everything the salesperson says. Keep the words and logic simple. If there's too much complexity, the shopper won't hook the talk of negative information to the salesperson's credibility.

The degree of shopper trust at the point of purchase determines your most promising selling strategy. Consider the situation in which the product or service you're offering can be customized with a range of optional add-ons. One way you might present such an item is to start with the bare-bones version and then offer suggestions for augmentations. Another way would be to start with the fully loaded model and then, if the shopper seems overwhelmed by the complexity or price, offer ideas for options which could be pruned out.

In either case, your recommendations are more likely to be accepted by the shopper if you precede your recommendations by probing with questions to learn about the shopper and how the shopper plans to use the item. This line of questioning provides you the information to deliver advice which is on-target for this individual consumer. It also means your recommendations will come across as credible.

When you do this and in other ways dispel any impressions that you're placing the interests of the store alone above those of the shopper, start with the bare-bones model and build up. However, if you sense that the shopper still doesn't trust your motives, you improve your chances of making a sale by promptly moving to consideration of the fully loaded model and suggesting what could be pruned. The take-off sequence results in higher average sales overall.

If the shopper has questions, it's sometimes best to eloquently answer the question you wished the customer had asked you rather than the question the customer actually asked.

People are quite likely to trust the advice of someone who answers a related question convincingly. There's a good chance the consumer will forget about the original question they were asking and will conclude that their question has been answered.

Consumers often feel a need to ask questions of a salesperson, especially if the shopper has to convince others the shopper is making a good decision. They think they'll be challenged by friends or family with, "Did you ask questions before you made that big purchase?" For this shopper, the importance is in the process of asking questions as much as in the specific content of the questions that are being asked.

The phenomenon is seen in how consumers who are expert in a product category handle technical specifications when making purchase decisions in that category. Experts ask for the specifications, but mostly want to know the answers so they can justify to themselves and others that they've made the right choices. Experts are notoriously complacent about using the technical information before choosing what they'll purchase.

On the other hand, the shopper might be markedly less familiar with the product than is the salesperson and therefore is less knowledgeable than the salesperson about what it's important to ask about. This shopper appreciates the salesperson's help in redirecting or rephrasing the question.

In asking the question, the shopper is wanting to build their confidence when making the purchase decision. Because the sharp salesperson is familiar with giving the answer to the question they wish they'd been asked, the salesperson can answer with the enthusiasm and fluency that projects confidence to the shopper.

Here are the steps to follow in order to answer the question you want to have been asked:

- Start by saying something like, "Thank you for your question."
- Give a general description of the question that allows a transition to what you want to answer. "You're asking me about...."
- Eloquently answer the question you wish you had been asked.
- After giving what you believe to be a sufficient answer, check with the shopper. Say, "Did I address your question?" This is better than, "Did I answer your question?"
- If the shopper says that you did not, request the customer to pose the question again. Then in your answer, stay closer to what the shopper is asking.

Once you take enough steps to establish and maintain trust, encourage satisfied customers to refer others to you. A referral builds trust in and loyalty to the retailer within the shopper who's referred and also within the customer who makes the referral. People yearn for connection, so links can be based on considerations having little to do with the product or service. For instance, when a customer finds they have the same birthday or place of birth as a salesperson, the customer gets more interested in making a purchase and is more likely to be satisfied with the purchases, the salesperson, and the retail establishment.

Researchers at University of British Columbia and INSEAD-Singapore[79] set up a study in which a personal trainer offered a fitness program to prospective enrollees. Participants who believed the fitness instructor was born on the same day as them became more likely to rate a sample program highly and to sign up for a membership. And dental patients who believed they were born in the same place as their dentist were more likely to rate their care highly and to schedule future appointments at that clinic. This effect is related to why chitchat at the start helps a sales pitch and, as described in Chapter 3, why pricing digits that match a shopper's birthdate garner good will.

Yet, overfamiliarity can hurt. What difference does it make if an individual salesperson or an ad for a store says, "Together, we can find what's best for you," instead of, "This store can find what's best for you"?

Researchers at University of Florida, Stanford University, and Turkey's Koç University[80] explored when, if ever, a misplaced "we" implies an intimacy which vexes shoppers. First, they created three versions of a Wells Fargo Bank ad to use in their studies. The difference was in the wording of one sentence:

- "Together, we make whatever decisions necessary to ensure your life goes uninterrupted."
- "Together you and Wells Fargo make whatever decisions necessary to ensure your life goes uninterrupted."
- "Wells Fargo makes whatever decisions necessary to ensure your life goes uninterrupted."

For current customers of the bank, the first version led to the most favorable attitudes. They liked the idea of the bank and the customer acting as if one. For non-customers, the outcome was more complex. In general, the wording made no difference. Non-customers had no psychological investment in the relationship with the bank, so probably weren't assessing the differences in the language. However, when another group of non-customers were specifically asked to pay attention to the differences, the "we" phrasing was less well received than the "you and Wells Fargo." It seems the "we" did portray a smarmy congeniality.

And then there are the businesses with whom even long-time customers don't expect to be chummy. In another part of the study, the researchers found that customers of health insurer Aetna were significantly more comfortable hearing a "you and Aetna" message than a "we" message.

Know what sort of retailer you are in the mind of the consumer. If it's expected that you'll maintain a professional distance to exercise independent judgment which can be trusted, this should be reflected in the marketing and face-to-face phrasing you use.

Celebrity referrals—going under the name "endorsements"—have influence if trusted. Good business judgment suggests that you don't want your celebrity endorser also praising your competition. But from the standpoint of believability, it doesn't hurt unless there are direct contradictions in the statements. People can like more than one store or merchandise brand in a retail category. If the celebrity endorser stops touting the competition and starts praising you, that equates to bonus points.

The closer the match between the celebrity image and the shopper's ideal self-image, the more effective is the endorsement. Recognize that the ability of the celebrity to violate expectations is sometimes what shoppers consider to be attractive because the shopper's ideal self would violate expectations. This argues for, with such consumers, using edgy celebrities and for featuring that edginess in ads. However, if the celebrity violates taboos, a continuing endorsement of your store or offerings can be damaging. During year 2010, marketing agency Zeta Interactive tracked how the value of Lance Armstrong's celebrity endorsements for RadioShack stores dropped precipitously as Mr. Armstrong's reputation for testing the limits turned into clear evidence he had used performance-enhancing drugs.

When your store or the brands you sell are presented with celebrity endorsements, the endorser's characteristics rub off on the product image. Endorsement from an individual makes you dependent on the behavior of that individual. If the endorsement is from a group—such as a sports team instead of a particular star on the team, you've more flexibility to craft the evidence: If one member of the group behaves improperly, you can feature another member of the group. With a sports team, if they're winning, you'll play on how your store or brands are winners. When the team is losing, you'll play on how your store and brands stay the course and keep getting better. Remember the underdog effect from Chapter 3?

Also, when the endorsement is from a group, the association is often at a deeper emotional level than when the endorsement is from an individual.

In my experience working with retailers, a source of endorsements even more profitable than celebrities is store staff. Become experts about what you sell so the recommendations to shoppers are well-founded. I've a caution, though: If shoppers ask the reasons for the recommendations, watch out the experts don't lie.

Product and service experts usually don't stay sufficiently familiar with details of their logic. They're accustomed to giving advice from habit rather than tracing out the details each time. If pinned down by requests for those details, experts often make up reasons for their conclusions. What's worse is that the experts tend to consider the reasons as genuine. They'll create false memories on the spot and then accept those memories as real. They don't know they're lying.

Staff members identified as experts are proud of the designation and feel accountable for advice they give. When they can't recall details in their reasoning, they assume it must have slipped from mind. They dig deeper to fill in the gaps, not realizing the deep digging leads their brains to subconsciously create phony recollections.

Lying to comparison shoppers, even with good intentions, is problematic when you're wanting to cultivate trust. Coach your staff to stay aware of their reasoning in giving recommendations. Encourage them to take the time to answer shopper questions to the point where each shopper is satisfied. Your salesperson may have heard this question hundreds of times, but for the shopper, it might be the first time the question has come up.

Distinguish solid recommendations from puffery. Puffery consists of lavish, often exaggerated, claims about a store or about products carried by the store. The U.S. Federal Trade Commission doesn't consider puffery to be illegal lying. That's because the FTC defines puffery as too subjective for the truth or falsity to be determined.

Sometimes what's said is obviously puffery: "We give the best store service you'll ever find." In other cases, the degree of puffery is harder for the consumer to spot because it consists of exaggerated importance placed on a trivial claim: "Our house brand ice cream uses only European flavors."

This second sort of puffery does build positive attitudes toward the store and other items carrying the brand name.

Should you engage in puffery? The effectiveness of the technique depends on the expertise of the shopper, the channel you use to deliver the message, and how you do the comparisons. Puffery is more likely to influence a consumer to buy a product when the consumer believes other people in general know more about the particular store or particular product category than they themselves do. It's also more likely to positively influence the consumer when delivered by a source the consumer considers to have expertise about shopping for products in the category they're considering.

If presenting the shopper a comparison of three—such as three products you carry—puffery about one of them will influence the shopper to favor that one, but the same puffery about a trivial attribute possessed by two of the three will drastically undercut any influence of the puffery.

A risk in using puffery is that consumers who are not positively influenced will lose trust in the retailer's other, validated claims of benefits. But if you've quality products to offer and maintain a staff with acknowledged expertise, expose shoppers to your puffery. Let the puffery demonstrate the abundant enthusiasm you and your staff have for what you're offering in your store. This, in turn, usually builds trust.

At the same time, watch out that the recommendations don't turn into a hard sell. I warn you that if you sell me, and people like me, too hard, I'll lose trust in you. That's why I cancelled my maintenance agreement with my HVAC (heating, ventilation, and air conditioning) company.

I say "my HVAC company" because I, like most consumers, feel an extra commitment to a retailer when subscribing to a company service. People agreeing to a flat-fee arrangement are especially likely to build commitment to the retailer and recommend the retailer to others if the customers are referred to as "members of the plan" rather than as "subscribers to the plan."

But I probably would have cancelled my enrollment and begun to look for another vendor even if I'd been called a member. The problem was I no longer trusted the retailer's interest in saving me money, and that was my motivation for enrolling in the first place.

Previous to all this, as I'd been seeking a new HVAC system, the company had been praised to me by a good friend. When the sales rep came, he asked me revealing questions about my needs and wants. The system he proposed seemed adequate for my specifications. He also described the alternatives and recommended against a more expensive system which he said was more than my house required.

I was impressed with the company's customer focus. When I received an e-mail encouraging me to enroll for the maintenance at a monthly fee, I did so promptly. About every six months, I got a call to schedule a visit, at no extra charge, to tune up the system. I liked the peace of mind. I could now think about things beyond whether the system needed maintenance. Psychological inertia set in, as it will for any customers you have on a flat-fee or subscription arrangement.

Then something changed for me. Each time, the serviceman came, he finished by suggesting some system improvement to be done at an additional cost. When I turned down a recommendation because the payback didn't seem adequate, on the next visit, there would be a different proposal for additional work. Every maintenance visit ended with the serviceman pressuring me to have more work done. My trust, which had started out strong, was evaporating.

This effect is related to the pushback of reactance, which I'll discuss in the next chapter. Still, it's not identical to reactance, since in this case I wanted to restore my confidence. That would be easier than having to find another HVAC company. Like most other consumers, I lust for trust in my service retailing relationships. So I telephoned the company and shared my impression that the list of recommendations was never-ending and that I was starting to doubt that the company was watching out for my best interests.

I'd have been comforted if the voice at the other end of the line had said something like, "I'll instruct the serviceman who comes out each time to give recommendations only if you ask." Or, "I'll ask the serviceman to suggest work to be done only when it's a matter of safety or there's a clear payback in energy costs he can describe to you. Our interest is in your safety, comfort, and savings."

Instead, her reply, with an impolite tone, was, "Well, you don't have to take the recommendations."

My suspicions were confirmed.

If you want to keep the trust and business of your customers, continually watch out for their best interests and let them know how diligently you're doing that.

RIMinders

- Point out to customers that you've kept your promises and how there have been benefits to them from this.

- An offer of a money-back guarantee will earn more trust when you state specific reasons you'll accept merchandise returns. An unconditional guarantee usually earns less shopper trust.

- When advertising money-back guarantees, place primary emphasis on the assurance that the purchased product will deliver on what's been promised. Place secondary emphasis on how the MBG insures that if anything goes wrong, the cost to make things right will be limited to getting the remnants of the merchandise back to you.

- A photo, even if related only indirectly to a claim you're making, often adds noticeably to the trust the listener places in that claim.

- Decide for yourself the circumstances under which you consider it ethically acceptable to sell a remedy that works only because the purchaser expects it to. Related to this, decide if and when you'll use puffery—lavish, often exaggerated, claims about a store or about products carried by the store.

- Unless your store brand already is widely trusted by your target audience, deliver any disclaimers at the same pace the body of the ad is delivered, and in the same tone of voice from the same announcer.

- Give shoppers what they need to make an informed decision. But be careful not to overload with information.

- Take the time to answer shopper questions to the point where each shopper is satisfied. When asked an uncomfortable question by a shopper, start by answering a related question you wish you'd been asked. But if that does not satisfy the shopper, maintain trust by answering in a way that stays close to what you've been asked.

- Let shoppers know ways in which you are similar to them. However, maintain a professional distance.

- With celebrity endorsements, the closer the match between the celebrity image and the shopper's ideal self-image, the more effective is the endorsement. More important than the likeability of the celebrity is a match between the nature of the product or service and the acknowledged expertise of the celebrity.

- See the advantages in endorsements from a well-known group or your own store staff rather than from a celebrity individual.
- People agreeing to a flat-fee arrangement—such as a maintenance service contract—are more likely to build commitment to the retailer and recommend the retailer to others if the customers are referred to as "members of the plan" rather than as "subscribers to the plan."
- Coach your staff to stay aware of their reasoning in giving recommendations.
- Shun the hard sell.

8

Control

⌒

"**I** am Dr. Fredrickson," the man began as he stepped through the curtain to address the audience. "I was called to this theatre half an hour ago, and I have just declared as deceased the female lead of the play you came to see tonight. The rest of the cast and the house management are in shock. They asked me to come out here to tell you."

Silently, the audience members stood up and, with one exception, moved toward the doors. The one exception, a short woman standing on her theatre seat to see above the exiting crowd, yelled out to Dr. Fredrickson, "Give her some chicken soup."

The doctor looked highly surprised. "She's deceased. Perhaps you didn't hear me."

"Go ahead and try some chicken soup," the short woman yelled back.

"Madam, the woman is dead. How could chicken soup help?"

"Well," replied the woman loudly, "it couldn't hurt."

Some might call that an overwhelming faith in chicken soup. I'll call it magical thinking. Shoppers want very much to feel in control of the situation, and in circumstances when consumers are striving to maintain that control, they might pull magic out of their hats. The results could be a superstitious failure to handle reality well. Or the magical thinking might make no difference at all, as in the case of Dr. Fredrickson's latest and late patient.

In reality, magical thinking might be so helpful to the consumer that the retailer is wise to go along. Acknowledge the power of magical thinking and how the sorts of shopper habits I discussed in Chapters 4 and 5 include what are best understood as superstitions.

Superstitions are most likely to influence consumers at times of uncertainty and when there is information overload. Because we're living in times of frequent worldwide economic uncertainty and because today's shoppers are exposed to monumental amounts of advertising and advice, we'd expect to see more shopper superstitions.

Use this fact to improve your profitability. The shopper's superstition might take the form of carrying good luck charms. For them, pair positive shopping experiences with a memory aid, such as small items carrying your store logo. Other shoppers might believe in the power of fate or karma regardless of what lucky charms they're packing.

Karma—which is associated with East Indian culture—is a belief system centered around long-term consequences. As we look forward in our lives, the decisions we make now affect what happens to us in the future. Good actions will produce good results at some point. Turning to look behind, we'll see that what is going on with us now is the result of our past—the thoughts we've had, the words we've said, the actions we've taken, the deeds we've instructed others to take on our account or while under our control.

This is seen as being true for everyone, since even the youngest child possesses a past, having lived a succession of existences. Universally, pleasant experiences will happen for us now because of good we've done in this or a former life. My unpleasant experiences are the consequences of my bad thoughts, words, and deeds in the past, according to the belief system of karma.

Researchers from Dartmouth College and Columbia University[81] concluded that consumers who believe in karma are more patient in resolving complaints about retailers than are consumers who don't believe in karma. The other side of this—since as with good and bad, there is always the other side—is that people who believe in karma are more persistent than those who don't. Even if they were to attribute bad customer service to their own past bad actions, they do not lower their expectations of good customer service. After all, these consumers want to see themselves as good, and one indicator that they've been good is that they finally receive good customer service from you.

When serving customers who identify with an East Indian cultural background and serving others who demonstrate a belief in karma, recognize the added importance of patience and persistence in resolving any customer service complaints.

Along with this, be 4-warned about what many American consumers would call superstition and certain consumers of Chinese, Korean, and Japanese heritage would call good judgment: The use of "4" in retail sales requires special caution. The Canon PowerShot G series went from G3 to G5, and there was never a Nokia cell phone series beginning with 4. Hong Kong hotels often don't have a fourth floor, and many Asian retailers avoid having a phone number which includes a 4.

The reason: Although in certain other parts of the world, four-leaf clovers have a reputation for good luck, in some Chinese dialects, the word for 4 is pronounced almost identically to the Chinese word for death. It's another example of the contagious magic I discussed with you earlier in the context of the extra value attributed to a tape measure used by Jackie Kennedy, a golf club swung by Ben Curtis, and gum chewed by Brittany Spears.

The consumer's urge for control also shows up in ways more subtle than superstitions. House brands, for instance. There's been a trend among retailers to use the same private label brand name across product categories. The reason is that these house brands have succeeded in establishing not only a price advantage over national supplier brands, but also a reputation for superior quality.

Private label items cost the customer, on average, about one-third less than the price of the national label brand. But in some categories, the private label item costs more than the average national label brand, and overall, the relative prices of the private label alternatives have been climbing.

When items carry the same brand name across product categories— such as a bath soap and a shampoo—you'd like to strengthen the brand image by using the same package design. Having almost identical package designs is common with house brands, where a consumer could be looking at pickle relish and party streamers during the same shopping trip.

Overall, using a similar package design to build brand image is a good idea from a shopper psychology perspective. Mere familiarity brings credibility, you'll recall.

There's a potential downside, though. When packaging is similar across items, the shopper senses a loss of control. The consequence might be that shoppers seek variety beyond the similarly branded items. The shopper becomes a bit less likely to buy the house brand across product categories unless you take steps to restore the sense of control.

Introduce distinctions by placing products with the same package design in different relative shelf positions for different product categories. With the mouthwash, the house brand is to the top left of the other brands, while with the toothpaste, the house brand is to the bottom right of the other brands. Also, use distinctive designs and color schemes on signage for different product categories. Such techniques give the shopper a sense of control, and this sense of control curbs further variety seeking.

In a University of Pennsylvania[82] study, participants were exposed to loud sirens, bells, and alarms. Some of the participants were allowed control over the amount of the anxiety-producing noise, while the rest were not.

Later, each of the participants was asked to express preferences between two sorts of items. Some of the items had borders; the others did not. For instance, the participant could choose a postcard to keep. The sole difference between the two cards was the thick border around one of the cards.

The study participants who had been granted no control over the anxiety-producing noise were more likely to select the postcard with the border around it. In subsequent experiments, people who felt little control preferred retail settings characterized as "highly bounded."

Circumstances in which your shoppers might feel especially anxious include:

- After experiencing—or maybe reading about—a disaster occurring close to them

- When coming into your store to solve a pressing problem involving loss or potential loss, such as after the death of a loved one or when a family member is seriously ill
- Toward the end of a paycheck cycle in a financially strained community

In these circumstances, here are a few research-based ways to fence in the consumer anxiety to make the shopping experience better:

- Keep shelves orderly and fully faced with items lined up neatly. That's like avoiding gaps in a fence.
- Regularly unclutter aisles. This doesn't necessarily mean to have wider aisles, though. Narrow without crowding is best.
- Establish time limits on sales promotions and return policies, and then remind customers of the time limits. "Please remember that this offer is good only for the next three days."
- Wherever shoppers need to wait, make it abundantly clear who has which place in line.
- Pose questions which remind shoppers of psychological boundaries they themselves have set. Ask, "How did you decide on the item with that brand name?," and then after listening to the answer, "Have you seen these new items we're introducing which carry that same brand name?"

At first glance, it might seem that setting additional limits would subtract from the shopper's sense of control and add to the shopper's anxiety. However, reasonable limits are reassuring.

Consumers who come shopping with a strong structure already in their lives have less need for the retailer to do the fencing. Let's return to those University of Pennsylvania study participants who had no control over the sirens, bells, and alarms. It turns out that those who had previously reported having strong religious beliefs were not as likely afterwards to select highly bounded items as were the other participants.

From the start of the shopping trip, give a sense of control to the shopper. Retailers of packaged goods should offer to each consumer entering the store both a shopping basket and a shopping cart. If a large shopping cart is the only carrying option greeting the customer, that customer could become annoyed. The person might intend to purchase only a few items and would prefer to use a shopping basket which is smaller and can be carried quickly by hand.

Offer the consumer options for when to complete the purchase. This gives a sense of control that can in itself ease stress. This works with advance scheduling, such as for dentist appointments. But it also can work when it comes to queuing up in the store. If the customer who is told, "I can check out your purchases over here," responds with, "I can wait," the store staff response should be an understanding nod rather than a puzzled or irritated look.

Beyond the point where you, the retailer, have set desired and reasonable limits on the shopper who seeks a sense of control, consumers react strongly against whatever they perceive as efforts to take their control away. If you put a whole bunch of sales pressure on a customer, they might rebel, becoming determined not to do what you're trying to convince them to do. They start debating each idea you present and physically distance themselves from you.

Reactance kicks in when shoppers sense that their freedom is threatened. In fact, a powerful store slogan sometimes causes consumers to do the opposite of what the retailer intended.

Researchers at University of Miami, University of California-Berkeley, and Hong Kong University of Science and Technology[83] presented people with a slogan in the spirit of freeing up spending: "Luxury. You deserve it." The researchers compared the effects against that from exposure to a spending-neutral slogan: "Time is what you make of it."

Those exposed to the luxury slogan decided to spend 26% less than those exposed to the neutral slogan. They rebelled against the intrusive urging in the slogan.

Does it work in the opposite direction? Yes. People exposed to "Dress for less" decided to spend 29% more than a matching group primed with the neutral slogan.

So suppose I ask your shoppers to think about the slogan "Save money. Live better," and then the slogan "The good life at a great price." You might recognize that the first of those slogans has been used by Walmart, and the second one by Sears. Both store names are associated with thriftiness. But I'm asking your shoppers to think about the slogans, not the store names.

The research team found that thinking about either of those slogans increased the amount of money people were willing to spend during a shopping trip. In fact, the amount was almost twice as much after thinking about the slogan than after thinking about the store name. With the store name, the average amount study participants were willing to spend was $94. With the slogan, it was $184.

Although knowing about reactance is important for retailers, it's even more important to know how to manage its onset. Doing this keeps your shoppers receptive to increasingly assertive sales appeals.

Your focus should always be on what helps your retail profitability, but achieve this by fulfilling the best interests of the customer. Then frame your sales pitch around these genuine benefits. Customer suspiciousness triggers reactance. On the other hand, reactance will be delayed if the shopper feels they owe the retailer for being helpful.

As soon as you see reactance developing, physically step back from the shopper for a brief time. Whenever possible, move to a less crowded shopping area or to an area in which there is a large selection of products. Crowded store spaces and limited product assortment heighten reactance, even when the shopper is seeking items of a different type.

You might encourage the shopper to back off, too. There are the habitual purchases which are quick and easy for the shopper. And there are the decisions—such as those requiring a change in brand or a large expenditure of time or money—which are difficult for the consumer. In these circumstances, people often put off the purchase and, if they do make the buy, they're often plagued with lingering doubts.

Consumer scientists at Cornell University and University of Toronto[84] suggest that when the shopper is feeling overwhelmed by a difficult decision, and you want to make the sale, you encourage the shopper to back off. Literally.

In one of their studies, the scientists presented consumers with two equally attractive products and invited the consumers to either choose one of the products right then or defer the decision. Next, some of the consumers were asked to lean in toward the computer screen where the products were displayed. The remaining group of consumers were asked to lean away from the computer screen.

Compared to those leaning away, those leaning in toward the screen reported the choice between the products to be more difficult and were more likely to ask to come back later.

The scientists found that it also worked for shoppers to cognitively lean away from the decision by thinking more abstractly. For instance, ask the shopper to think about ways the two products are alike.

Other studies find that a similar advantage can be achieved by encouraging a confused consumer to go on to another entry on the shopping list and then come back in a short while to make the purchase decision.

Note that the effects of physical or imagined approach and avoidance are different when it comes to building the appeal of a specific item rather than the act of choosing between two items.

In a University of Chicago and University of Arizona project,[85] student participants were shown a can of food. The label on the can announced that the contents consisted of curried grasshopper, an item most of the students instantly decided would make a poor lunch choice. The students were not, however, averse to eating for pay.

Some of the students were then asked to imagine themselves avoiding the can, and afterwards instructed to eat the curried grasshopper and report their evaluation. Another group was asked to imagine themselves approaching the can before they received the eating and evaluation instructions.

The participants who imagined approach beforehand gave the more positive evaluations.

Encourage approach in building attraction, then allow temporary withdrawal to ease indecision.

The extent of reactance does depend on the nature of the item for sale. Researchers at Georgetown University and Ben-Gurion University[86] were intrigued by the success of the Nike slogan, "Just Do It," which is highly directive.

The researchers found that highly directive sales messages do not trigger reactance if the products or services bring happiness. The happiness might come from immediate sensual pleasure. The salesperson for the day spa appointment says, "You belong on our massage table." Or the happiness might come from an anticipated sense of accomplishment. Running the marathon in Nike shoes qualifies under that prong.

Contrast this with what would happen at a bank where the staff want to store your money. In the study, some participants read a message encouraging them to try a chocolate treat. The other participants' message encouraged them to open a bank account.

Those in the first condition responded best to an assertive message, "You must try our chocolate." Those with the bank message responded best to a non-assertive pitch, "You could open a bank account with us." This is consistent with what was found in the study of Wells Fargo Bank messages I presented in Chapter 7.

When the researchers analyzed slogans for retail products, they found that 24% of successful hedonic products—such as ice cream, beer, and designer jeans—have assertive slogans. Among successful utilitarian products—real estate and diapers, for instance—the percentage was only 8%.

Never push the customer too hard. Otherwise you'll push them away from this sale and future sales at your store. However, at any point where what you're selling is pleasure, up the assertiveness. Be sure you're convinced this is the right purchase decision for this shopper. Then, with justified confidence, let them know why you are convinced.

With the most assertive sales pitches, still acknowledge the consumer's ability to choose. Giving choices gives control. In the spirit of choice-building control, "I don't" works better than "I can't" for consumers young and old. In most of our interactions with consumers, we're wanting them to do something. Still, there are many retailers of services who succeed when they empower a client not to do something. The clearest examples are in the treatment of habit disorders, such as at clinics for weight loss or substance abuse. A starting point in the treatment is for the client to sincerely conclude that the existing consumption habit needs to be changed and can be changed. Addictive behaviors are another instance of the sorts of examples I catalogued in Chapter 4 where we want to ease the switching costs.

Toward this end, how do we build up the resistance to temptation? Researchers at University of Houston and Boston College[87] say that a change of phrase can help: Teach the client to say, "No, I don't," when faced with the temptation.

Study participants were assigned to one of three groups, based on which statement they were instructed to say to others and to themselves:

- "No, I won't"
- "No, I can't"
- "No, I don't"

Over the course of the study, each participant received a daily e-mail with a reminder of what to say. The participants were also asked to regularly report details of circumstances in which the phrase worked or didn't work, along with the feelings and thoughts experienced.

The "No, I don't" group reported substantially more success in resisting temptations than did those in the other two groups. They also said they noticed improvements in feelings of self-direction. They became more likely to believe and act as though they themselves were making the decision to decline than that somebody else was forcing them to do it.

An adaptation of this technique can be used regarding salesperson-shopper interactions. When a consumer makes a request that is unrealistic, we are better off saying, "My store does not do that," rather than, "My store won't do that" or "My store can't do that."

Notice that in this case, none of the statements would begin with, "No." This is because "no" is a shopper's least favorite word. Along with the avoidance of "not," for which I advocated in Chapter 1, our general rule is to eschew "no." Instead, develop a way to say "yes, if" by setting a price on acceptably satisfying the person.

When you do need to say no, accompany the no with a yes. The dieter should be sure what to eat in addition to what not to eat. The substance abuser should know what, when facing temptation, is the productive thing to do and why to do this, along with what not to do and why. For instance, you could hit them with the possibility that if they eat the wrong foods or habitually abuse drugs, they'll die sooner. Recall that possibilities carry more weight than probabilities with consumers.

Of course, the true state of possibility is that we are all going to die. The probabilities have to do with how soon. As it happens, people confronted with the certain possibility of their mortality spend more money at retailers. During a natural disaster, when consumers are hearing about widespread causalities, they'll stock up on emergency supplies. But after the dust settles, they'll go for the indulgences over the necessities. Consumer psychologists used findings like these as they developed what's now called Terror Management Theory.

TMT studies find that the urge to splurge sets in after the extreme fear passes. The motivation to buy comes from a desire to increase self-esteem, since self-esteem gives a sense of control. The colloquial phrase "I was so embarrassed I could've died" reflects a relationship between threats to self-esteem and one's demise. Therefore, your selling message is that the purchase will help shoppers feel better about themselves.

Researchers at University of London and Cornell University[88] gave 150 study participants information designed to temporarily threaten the participants' self-esteem. One consequence was that the amount participants were willing to pay for fancy cars, luxury watches, and other high-status goods climbed. The agreeable amount stayed pretty much the same for non-status items. By comparison, the amount people were willing to pay for high-status goods did not climb in the absence of threats to self-esteem.

Because different people have different sources of self-esteem, they'll seek different items. Researchers at Stanford University and Duke University[89] had women think about a terrorist attack and then choose a reward of either chocolate cake or fruit salad. Among those who had previously said their body image contributed greatly to their self-esteem, thinking about the terrorist attack increased the frequency of selecting the fruit salad by 15 percentage points. But among those who had previously said their self-esteem came from considerations other than their body image, thinking about the terrorist attack increased the frequency of selecting the cake by 50 percentage points.

What this means to you as a retailer is that whenever you raise a shopper's self-esteem from a low level, you're appealing to an especially deep and compelling need in that shopper for control over the inevitable. Since consumers associate self-esteem with items having social status, the effectiveness of self-esteem appeals is greatest with status items. To maximize the effectiveness of that motivation, make it a point to remind shoppers to enjoy themselves before it's too late. Also give genuine and generous praise whenever the shopper purchases a luxury item. I recommend you build the self-esteem after the purchase is made. When praise is given before the purchase, the urge to splurge fades.

Is it morally right to take advantage of people's desires for merchandise if they're shopping because of a fear of death? In my opinion, it's fine to deliver value by relieving your customers' anxiety. The three caveats for me are: Don't violate the law to make customers feel good. Don't gouge people by charging excessive prices. Don't pressure people to buy when they're seeming to struggle with temptation.

Those are my rules. What are yours?

Again, a caveat regarding young consumers: TMT motivation is reserved for adults. Reminding children they'll inevitably die is nothing if not ghoulish. And teenagers—those reckless rascals—already too often behave and misbehave on the assumption they'll never die.

With or without a fear of death, consumers usually feel in greater control when shopping decisions are on the simple side. Researchers at UCLA and Israel's Interdisciplinary Center Herzliya [90] found that interest in enrolling in a retirement savings program involving some risk was increased by asking the consumer an easy instead of a difficult question about finance. Further, when people were given an abundance of technical information about a particular mutual fund, the people reported a drop—not a climb—in their subjective knowledge, and thereby became less willing to invest in that fund.

Being flooded with information made people less confident and more wary. We saw in Chapter 7 how information overload corrupts informed decisions. In the UCLA/Herzliya studies, caution arose when investment prospects were reminded of what they did not know about the mutual fund, again decreasing the self-reported subjective knowledge. Our impression of what we know—our subjective knowledge—is often more important in consumer decision making than is our actual, objective level of knowledge.

We'd like our customers to feel confident about their purchases. Yet we don't want customers making misinformed investment decisions or misusing what they buy. We'd prefer our patrons to be not only confident, but also what consumer psychologists call "well-calibrated." In well-calibrated customers, the discrepancy between subjective knowledge and objective knowledge is small. Any shopping confidence is deserved. With financial decisions, calibrate consumers by providing them tools to play around with various scenarios at their own pace.

Also remember to balance necessary complexity with the allure of simplicity. Clothing retailer Lucky Brand redesigned stores as part of a simplification initiative. Whatever fashions were shown in the display windows outside the store were stocked close to the front door for easy pickings. Whole outfits were displayed together for those fashionistas who question their eye-eye coordination. Upper shelves inside the store were used for display rather than for holding merchandise, cutting down on the need to stretch the body while stretching the budget.

Still, Lucky Brand discovered that what's simple for one type of shopper may seem needlessly complicated for another type. The women preferred to have jeans displayed on hangers for easier imagination of the look on the body, while the men wanted jeans stacked on shelves for more quickly locating the suitable size and cut.

If you implement this tactic, also keep in mind the findings I discussed in Chapter 2 about shoppers giving more positive evaluations to products that had been pushed back on the shelves rather than being in easy reach. Again, balance simplicity with challenge.

Providing the shopper a sense of control gets more complex when it involves a succession of decisions rather than a single one. Pretend you're planning a trip. Which flight to take? Where to rent the car? What hotel to stay at?

Flight. Car rental. Hotel. That might be the order in which you'll use the services, but researchers at Stanford University and Columbia University[91] wanted to see what happened when the order was changed around. How do the number of alternatives interact with the choice order in the speed of consumers' decisions and the comfort of the decision makers?

The researchers asked study participants to choose one each from among five flight options, fifteen car rental arrangements, and ten hotels. But the order of the three choices was varied for different groups of the participants.

It turned out that the choice of the hotel was quicker when it followed the choice among the fifteen rental cars than when it followed the choice among the five flights. Why was this, and how can you put this finding to use with your shoppers?

The explanation is that the consumers faced with selecting one from among fifteen options were overwhelmed by the possibilities, so adopted a "good enough" mindset. Others have called it "satisficing." With this mindset, the consumers make the choice of the hotel relatively quickly.

On the other hand, those consumers who started with the filtering of five options could hold out for "find the best," a form of perfectionism. When they moved on to the hotel choice, that approach caused them to spend more time on the task. Researchers refer to this as "maximizing," and maximizing can freeze consumers into indecision. Once you get into either a satisficing or maximizing frame of mind, you'll tend to shop that way for the rest of your store visit.

I could explain the finding a little differently: It's more tiring to choose among fifteen alternatives than among five. Making purchase decisions takes energy. Therefore, those who started out with the fifteen-alternative task didn't have as much perseverance when they got to the hotel task, so they got it over with quickly. An implication is that if the study participants had been given a brief break before moving on to the hotel choice, they would have taken the time to do it more carefully.

Whichever explanation you choose, if you want to encourage satisficing in your shopper, begin with the more complex decisions among alternatives and then promptly move on through the other choices to be made, leaving your customer feeling in control.

The sense of control that comes from perfectionism is a tougher nut to crack. Perfectionist shoppers are a nuisance for retailers. They consume an abundance of your time to conclude a sale and then might return items or resist paying for a service because their unrealistic expectations were not fulfilled.

There's a large genetic component in perfectionism. A person's environment—the strictness of a parent's standards, the reactions of bosses to errors on the job—shape the personality trait. But a larger determination comes from what you're born with. This means perfectionism is challenging to change.

It can be done, however, at least for the duration of the consumer's visit to your store. Start by determining if this shopper is, in fact, a true perfectionist rather than somebody who wants to fulfill a fantasy of having you as a slave to their whims. Is the shopper spiraling in toward a defined goal, even though that purchase goal is unattainable? A yes answer indicates you're dealing with a perfectionist. But if the demands change willy-nilly, and no matter what you do, you can't move toward a sale, terminate the harassment.

If it's truly perfectionism, identify areas important to the shopper for which you can satisfy their specifications completely or very close to completely. When other areas of concern keep coming up, evaluate how vital these would be for a non-perfectionist to receive full value from the transaction with you. It's likely you'll conclude it's fine for the shopper to satisfice. Then say how close you can come to what the perfectionist is asking you and bring the discussion back to the areas where you can indeed give perfection.

Handling perfectionist tendencies is another arena in which, although simplicity usually reigns, there are circumstances when you should complicate choice in order to satisfy a shopper's need for control. Among these circumstances are purchase decisions the consumer considers as having potentially life-changing consequences and the alternatives are quite clear-cut. Some of these situations, such as buying a house, extend over time. Others, such as selecting funeral arrangements, could last no more than a day or two.

These types of decisions have to do with people's careers, homes, caretakers, and life partners. Because of the significance of such choices, the person believes they should devote time and mental effort even if the process seems at first to constitute a straightforward selection.

In these circumstances, rather than help the consumer find shortcuts, tolerate how the consumer adds complexity:

- She focuses on the choice that does seem clearly best, but then exaggerates the importance of what are actually insignificant disadvantages of that choice.

- He changes the criteria for decision making he had previously decided to use so that the decision making has to start over.

- She keeps the same criteria, but agonizes over the relative weighting.

Resist pressuring the shopper or reassuring that the decision really is an easy one. A better alternative is to acknowledge to the shopper the significance of the decision and reflect, without criticism, on the convolution the shopper has introduced. You'll be complicating, rather than simplifying, the lifestyle choice in order to help the consumer satisfy a need for control.

To make your point even more effective, use formal language, such as, "Decisions like this are very important, so I fully understand your exploring all sides. You're starting the decision making process again so you can look at each part in detail. That will take the time and mental energy you want to put into this highly significant task."

RIMinders

- Analyze how the culture of your consumer influences shopping characteristics. For example, when serving customers who identify with an East Indian cultural background, recognize the added importance of patience and persistence in resolving any customer service complaints. Consumers from a Chinese, Korean, or Japanese heritage tend to avoid the use of the number 4 in retail transactions. Highly religious shoppers are willing to yield control to retailers who have earned their trust.
- For retail businesses such as weight loss and substance abuse programs, which are selling impulse control, teach clients to say "I don't" more than "I can't" or "I won't."
- Increase the consumer's deserved confidence in making financial decisions by providing the consumer tools to play around with various scenarios at their own pace.
- Remind shoppers to enjoy themselves before it's too late. Give genuine and generous praise whenever the shopper purchases a luxury item.
- In selling items that are more utilitarian than pleasure-oriented, avoid highly directive pitches.
- To help sidestep wasteful perfectionism in your customers, begin with the more complex decisions among alternatives and then promptly move on through the other choices to be made.

- To handle stubborn perfectionism in a shopper, say how close you can come to what the perfectionist is asking you and bring the discussion back to the areas where you can indeed give perfection.
- In circumstances where your shoppers are likely to feel anxious—such as right after a natural disaster—keep your store shelves orderly and fully faced with items lined up neatly.
- With purchase decisions the consumer considers as having potentially life-changing consequences and the alternatives are quite clear-cut, allow the consumer to introduce complexity, even if it strikes you as unnecessary.
- As soon as you see sales resistance developing, physically step back from the shopper for a brief time. Whenever possible, move to a less crowded shopping area or an area in which there is a large selection of products. Verbally step back by softening your arguments.
- Offer the customer options for when to complete the purchase.
- If shoppers need to wait, make it clear who has what place in line.
- Avoid saying "no" to a shopper. Instead, develop a way to say "yes, if" by setting a price on acceptably satisfying the person.

9

Personalization

~

Why did the Lutheran minister like to build brick walls for his family of parishioners?

I'm sure that, lurking somewhere, there's an uproarious answer to that riddle. However, the answer from the Lutheran minister I'm referring to was more thought-provoking pun than gut-busting laughter. When I asked, he replied that he liked to build brick walls because the creative construction was concrete. It was a change from his usual days carrying out religious duties, in which his results were harder to keep in place.

Some other men would have different motivations for brickwork—different benefits they received from doing it. Since retailers sell benefits, it's useful for us to know what all the attractions are for the range of shoppers we serve. Researchers at California State University-Long Beach, University of Nebraska, and Bath University[92] expanded this query beyond building brick walls to the overall Do-It-Yourself (DIY) home projects market.

The researchers discovered that an important determinant of consumer motivation is social class. Family men of relatively high social class with more resources in their lives often are drawn to the relief from knowledge work, a relief achieved as they work with their hands. These consumers consider DIY projects as leisure activities to be relished, never rushed. They'll browse at stores and introduce artistry into their projects as a form of personal expression.

Family men of lower social class with fewer resources in their lives often view the residence as an extension of the workplace. They're responsible for maintenance, and good stewardship means saving money by doing repairs and improvements yourself. Artistry in the DIY's projects will benefit the family by distinguishing their family from others that have limited resources and from the routine life to which many families of limited means are consigned.

The researchers' conclusion that consumers' motivations range along a dimension is a good reminder, but it is a conclusion already well-known by retailers. More useful is the researchers' insight that at both ends of the dimension, and therefore probably all along it, consumers seek to express themselves as artists. Handmade craftsmanship for all sorts of do-it-yourselfers gives a backstory the consumer can tell to family and friends who see the creation.

In what ways and to what ends are you helping your shoppers fulfill their personalized passions for artistic expression?

And another question for you, this one derived from a completely different research project: Why were people discarding good products?

Researchers at University of British Columbia and University of Alberta[93] spotted a clue in other actions the consumers under study were taking: The consumers were also customizing what appeared to be a flawless product or bringing it back to the store to make an exchange. It turned out that the products were not, in the person's opinion, perfectly flawless, after all. The flaw was that someone similar had the identical product. These consumers feared conformity.

Among triggers which set off a drive for distinctiveness are these:

- **Choice sequence.** Researchers from Sorbonne-Assas in France and University of Adelaide in Australia[94] found that, in a French restaurant, when 30% to 80% of a group had ordered the same choice, people placing their orders next tended to go along with also ordering this choice for themselves. But once the conformity exceeded 80%, subsequent orders were more likely to show variety seeking.
- **Age.** In most cultures, older shoppers are more likely to seek distinctiveness than conformity, while teenagers tend to opt for conformity with groups they aspire to belong to. Older consumers are

more fearful of conformity with fashion items, such as clothing and entertainment products. They're less concerned regarding functional items, like appliances and foods.

- **When product choice is thought to reveal personality characteristics.** In a project at University of Toronto, Hong Kong University of Science and Technology, and Sun Yat-sen University,[95] participants were urged to feel proud for a reason. With some, the reason given was what they had done. For others, the reason was that the day was worth enjoying. For the rest, the reason was who they were. Then, as a reward, each participant was offered a T-shirt. Three of the shirts were white and the fourth was red. The participants who had been urged to feel proud because of who they were selected the red shirt much more often than did the participants given one of the other reasons for pride.

- **Substantial effort by the shopper in making the product selection.** The effect of personality characteristics match is greater than that of substantial effort. As I discussed in Chapter 3, this is especially true when it comes to the expression of values. Still, people come to believe that if what they've done as a consumer was hard, they deserve a badge of distinction as recognition. In the Chapter 2 example of the potato chips in the hard-to-open bag, difficulty bestowed value. What the fear-of-conformity research adds is that the consumer will seek that value via distinctiveness.

When your shoppers do fear conformity, look for ways you can offer even minor variations in even mundane product lines. I've seen it work to have a choice of face plates on a mobile phone or alternative patterns on a wrist band.

Your shoppers will appreciate the chance to customize. What they'll like still more is the opportunity to personalize. Personalization goes beyond customization, in that personalization takes into account the characteristics of the particular individual. People love to put their personal imprint on their purchases. Most consumers choose to personalize even if it means accepting design quality inferior to what professional designers would produce.

For you, as a retailer, to personalize for shoppers, you need to open up each shopper enough to gather information. There's a series of exchanges about preferences, availability, substitutability, and more.

A prime use for any personalization information is in guiding a shopper through what may seem on the surface to be a contradiction: Shoppers who are aiming to satisfy a need are attracted by an abundance of choices to start with, but as they get closer to wanting to make a purchase decision, they welcome a pruning down of variety. They prefer a smaller, not a larger, assortment to assess. An abundance of alternatives attracts shoppers at the start, but, unless handled properly, decreases purchase momentum and shopper satisfaction.

Columbia University and Stanford University[96] researchers had found that shoppers presented with six choices of jam to sample from were less likely to take a sample than those offered 24 choices, but among those who did the sampling, those having been offered the six choices were ten times as likely to end up purchasing a jar of jam as were the shoppers presented with 24 choices.

Then in a followup study, participants were exposed to either six different varieties of Godiva chocolates or 30 different varieties. Those exposed to the lower number of choices were much more likely to subsequently select a box of Godiva chocolates rather than a cash payment for participation in the study.

Researchers at University of Chicago and Korea University[97] realized that consumers are more likely to buy an umbrella when it's raining than when it's sunny. You see, those researchers were a good cut above the proverbial absent-minded professor who wouldn't know to come in out of the rain if lacking an umbrella. What intrigued the researchers was how to effectively get consumers to select among a broad variety of umbrellas when the consumer feels overwhelmed by all the choices.

The answer was to present the choice to the consumer as an opportunity for expressing their distinctiveness. The right questions included, "What's important to you when selecting among umbrellas?" and later, "I'm interested in what led you to select this one over the others." Research participants were similarly more likely to make choices regarding vacation packages, literary novels, and flower bouquets when the choice process was framed as an opportunity to express themselves.

In your advertising, point out that you offer a large number of alternatives. When the person starts their shopping with you, display categories within categories to highlight the abundance of alternatives.

But then recognize the potential for information overload. To make things easier for the shopper, use similar wording in describing the features of each product or service. Provide tables that list features across the top, the names of a small selection of item alternatives along the left side, and checkmarks in the cells to indicate which item has which features.

In the product or service descriptions and in the table, list features concisely. Then outside the table, state the benefit of each feature: "Low rolling resistance gives you better fuel efficiency."

Limit to five both the number of important features and the number of product or service alternatives you want the shopper to consider. An exception to this is if the alternatives are very similar in what features they have. In this case, add one or two trivial features that one or two of the alternatives have, but the others don't. This helps unfreeze the decision maker who is immobilized by information overload.

Make it easy to choose more than one alternative. Say something like, "You've probably noticed this sweater comes in five designs. How many of those designs do you want to buy?" In signage, list the flavors along with text reading, "How many flavors would you like?" Offer a discount for multiple-item purchases. Set a package price that results in a lower per-item cost, such as six pairs of socks, two each of the three most popular colors.

Business-to-business shoppers might do a comprehensive objective weighted analysis of each product by feature. But as I said with the car airbag example in Chapter 1, the vast majority of shoppers will end up making a purchase as much on intuitive emotion as on the basis of scientific analysis. In fact, this usually results in better decisions because the intuitive emotion is driven by the individual shopper's personalized values. Therefore, there is a risk in you probing too much for reasons once the customer has made a decision. Excessive probing disrupts intuitive reasoning. Recall that if you ask a consumer to generate loads of reasons to buy a particular product or to shop at your store, the task becomes more difficult for the customer, and this actually makes their preferred alternative less attractive to them.

The advantages of funneling down choices are also seen with shoppers who are working toward a goal over time, such as a fitness program, a diabetes maintenance program, or physical rehabilitation from a serious injury. At the start of the program, the merchant or professional should offer the customer a broad variety of assistance items. Then as the customer feels closer to achieving the goal, offer a more limited selection based on personalization to the consumer.

In one University of Maryland study,[98] researchers asked each of a set of college students to write down an individual fitness goal. Next, some of the study participants were given evidence they were close to reaching the goal, while others were led to believe they were far from the goal.

All the participants were then shown a set of six protein items. In some cases, the items were all protein bars differing only in flavor. Six different flavors. This was a low-variety set. The other participants—some who felt close to their goal and some who felt far from it—were presented a high-variety set that included a protein bar, a protein shake, and four other forms of protein supplement. Six different forms. As a last step in the study, each participant was measured on their motivation to achieve the fitness goal.

The results: Among consumers who felt far from the goal, motivation was higher when the consumer was asked to choose among the high-variety set. On the other hand, among consumers who felt close to the goal, motivation to achieve the goal was higher when the consumer was asked to choose among the low-variety set.

Based on findings like these, the researchers suggest the retailer offer the goal-seeker a broad variety of assistance items at the start and then, as the customer feels closer to achieving the goal, offer a more limited selection.

With a self-help group working together toward a goal, the funneling from lots to little variety works best when the group feels they are all at a similar progress point. You could facilitate this by encouraging group members to take responsibility for each other's progress.

There's also another stream of consumer research showing the relationship between funneling the choices and meeting shoppers' desire for personalization. It has to do with creativity.

A classic exercise to develop individual creativity is to give someone a few objects—like a paper clip, a facial tissue, and a scrub brush—and ask the person to list all the different ways the objects could be used together. The assumption is that this task—using all the objects together—would be more difficult with, let's say, six objects than with, let's say, three. But does this mean that the six-objects task develops more creativity than the three-objects task?

No, according to researchers at New York University-Stern and University of British Columbia.[99] Their conclusion is that if shoppers have fewer options available—a smaller number of paint options for a decorating project or a smaller number of alternatives for preparing a dinner—creativity increases.

When shoppers are making purchase decisions that they believe express their personal values, they're happier if they believe they're exercising creativity. It appears that you can help your customers do this by progressively limiting their choices as they move toward a purchase decision. This finding fits with other evidence that a well-organized store encourages customer creativity, as long as it's not overdone. As we saw in Chapter 6, consumers do require sufficient complexity to stay engaged.

All this is more true for consumers who are highly experienced in combining the merchandise to meet objectives—the confident amateur interior decorators and chefs, for instance. Experts feel a greater need to evaluate all the available alternatives than do the novices, who want to keep things manageable. With an abundance of choices, the experts become anxious, which can immobilize creativity and, therefore, the consumer's feelings of having personalized the selection.

When it comes to cultivating creativity, a further step is important: Point out to the customer evidence of creativity. Restricted choice increased shopping enjoyment and *objective* creativity for experienced consumers. But the restricted choice often decreased the *subjective feelings* of creativity expressed by those consumers. Except if their creative output was pointed out to them.

In summary, the sell-well motivation of customization is accompanied at the start by having a broader assortment available. Then as the shopper moves closer to becoming a purchaser, use their desire for a personalized solution to funnel down the choices.

Reason-to-buy questions help the shopper consider their values, in turn increasing your opportunities to influence them. Asking these questions personalizes the selling arguments. People make each purchase decision for all sorts of reasons, and each of us has a distinctive consumer personality. Some shoppers primarily want to play it safe while others primarily want to acquire new advantages. The shopper can take your reason-to-select questions in whatever direction fits them best.

Shoppers in a marketing atmosphere filled with fears of privacy being violated will usually volunteer information about themselves to a retailer if they see the retailer using this to personalize the shopping experience. In truth, though, there are sensitive areas where the candor is less than what the retailer would find useful in selling well. People may be ashamed to reveal to you certain sorts of information that would help you know this particular shopper better.

Employ a five-step research-based sequence to increase the shopper's candor with you about sensitive topics:

- Start by establishing rapport with the shopper. In a setting where there is adequate privacy, ask questions which aren't sensitive.

- Next, give a few instances of sensitive information shoppers have shared with you in the past. For instance, a salesperson intending to help a shopper for a personal hygiene item might say, "Last month, a customer helped me zero in on the right product for them by describing a foot odor problem they were having." Be sure to protect the identity of the past customers. You certainly don't want to leave this shopper with the impression that you'll tell their secrets to others with a name attached. Instead, your objective is to increase comfort in sharing sensitive information with you because you've heard it all before.

- Ask the intrusive question in the form, "May I ask you….?" This is a yes-no—closed-ended—question. If it's not clear why the question you're asking about asking arises from your desire to offer a personalized solution to the shopper, explain why. Say, "Here's why I'd find your answer helpful in giving you the products and services which will best fit you."

- If the shopper grants you permission to ask the intrusive question, be ready to remember what you're told. If the shopper seems uncomfortable with your question, follow up with a somewhat less intrusive question. If the shopper answers that one, give the more intrusive question another try.

• When the transaction is complete, thank the shopper for helping you by giving you the sensitive information, and assure the customer you will protect their confidentiality. You've now formed a bond with the person, transforming them from a customer into a client.

Sometimes you don't need to ask about sensitive topics. When you spot social trends, you can offer customized items and then, when shoppers come in, personalize.

For instance, want to make some fast money off all those folks who are getting divorced? Sound too much like preying on others' misery? Well, done the wrong way, yes. But think instead about satisfying shoppers who can use what you provide as they set up their own housekeeping. In January 2010, Debenhams, with its 153 department stores located across the UK and Ireland, announced the inauguration of the Debenhams Divorce Gift Registry.

What products and services could you profitably provide to the newly divorced? Before deciding on implementation, though, consult the right statistics. You're interested in the percentage of your target market who are newly divorced or have filed for divorce. That's not the same as the percentage of marriages that end in divorce. Countries with the highest percentage of the population who get divorced include the U.S. and UK. At the other extreme, Brazil, Italy, and Mexico have very low rates. And the rates differ significantly within a country.

If you start a gift registry, include some high-end items. Friends of the divorced will want to soothe the suffering. Even the ex-mate might want to splurge on a present. A spouse who feels responsible for a breakup might be open to "compensatory giving."

If you advertise specifically to a divorce-ready market, be aware that some in your community will fault you, claiming you are encouraging divorce. The Presbyterian Church in Northern Ireland responded to the Debenhams announcement by calling it "very bizarre." Allow for dignity. Hallmark Cards has items for the newly divorced with text like "going through a difficult time." Still, Hallmark also put out a card reading, "Want to get rid of that ugly fat? Divorce him."

Debenhams has marketed to other niches. They were among the first British department store to showcase fashions using UK size 16 mannequins. This when nearly all clothing shops in Britain used size 8 or 10 mannequins.

At a time when a majority of American women would be classified as overweight by U.S. Centers for Disease Control and Prevention standards, only about 9% of retail revenues for women's clothing came from sales of plus sizes.

For men, the stigma against larger is smaller. Men buy "Big Dogs" T-shirts. And shops selling men's apparel can put "Big" in the store name without alienating shoppers, while retailers selling plus-size women's clothing stick with code words like "Lane Bryant."

Still, some men do hesitate. So there are retailers labeling trousers as a smaller size than the trousers really are. Debenhams, Next, and Topman in Great Britain were selling pants up to one inch larger than labeled. The objective was to have customers say, "I feel better about myself when shopping at that store rather than elsewhere, so I'll make more of my purchases there."

Car companies are positioning pedals farther apart. Not to be left behind, toilet seat makers are enlarging sizes. Airlines sell extra legroom and elbow room. After noticing that feet are getting bigger, Nordstrom Rack, Barefoot Tess, and Designershoes.com began offering shoes in sizes up to 15.

Profit awaits retailers who help their customers achieve physical comfort when using fashionable purchases. But the measures to achieve this are not always the same as measures taken to make customers feel emotionally comfortable about shopping for larger sizes. Debenhams realized that what they were doing was a test. Next to the first set of larger size mannequins were signs reading, "I'm a size 16. Do you want to see more of me?"

Overall, consumer psychology findings suggest that shoppers enjoy seeing items modeled by people who are somewhat thinner, although not dramatically thinner, than they themselves are. Researchers at Tilburg University and Arizona State University[100] found that when female study participants looked at moderately heavy models, the study participants began having unpleasant thoughts about their own weight. On the other hand, when the researchers showed images of moderately thin women, the viewers' self-esteem improved. Better self-esteem generated by an ad makes people more likely to absorb and act on the advertising message.

Still, also recognize the full content of the message. Stocking larger sizes, even if you don't show the items on mannequins, parallels having special sales days for senior citizens. The recipient of your message thinks, "This retailer recognizes my distinctive characteristics. I enjoy the pride in myself this shows me, so I'll want to give this store my business."

In the past, the most powerful selling to lesbian, gay, bisexual, and transgendered consumers has assumed that these consumers felt they were stigmatized by broader society. Retail establishments identified themselves as specifically catering to LGBTs as target markets. Businesses and individuals sported pink or rainbows in order to say, "We support you in spite of you being different."

Actually, consumers are getting more interested in being different rather than conforming to group preferences. You'll increase sales when you help your shoppers reach their favorite spot on the conformity-distinctiveness scale. A tool you have for doing this is the phrasing of certain preferences questions. These questions are the consumer counterparts to my Chapter 1 discussion of retailer projection, introjection, and marketing to the mirror.

If you ask your customer, "What about this product do you like that your friends would also like?," this prompts individual distinctiveness, since it puts your customer in the role of advisor and perhaps opinion leader.

On the other hand, if you ask your customer, "What about this product do your friends like and you also like?," this prompts the customer to think about the comfort of adhering to group preferences.

The desire for personalization can manifest itself in odd ways: Consumers generally strive to purchase and display items they associate with social classes they look up to. If a teen idol claims to use a certain brand of mobile device, other teens are motivated to get it, too. If a highly successful business leader appears at conferences with a briefcase showing a specific brand name and style, sales of those briefcases can be expected to climb among new MBAs.

Yet, there are circumstances under which consumers will strive to acquire items they associate with a lower socioeconomic status. Consumer psychologists call it "parody display." Your shoppers might know it as the related phenomenon of "slumming." Among Americans, tattoos were more popular in low socioeconomic classes before the prevalence moved uptown. Among Brazilians, capoeira—an art form that combines dance with martial arts and had its origins among slaves from Africa—was done most often in the slums before upper classes took it on as a form of parody display. Blue jeans. Pickup trucks. Work boots. And on and on.

Behind parody display might be a wish to relax. Your customers could be sick from "affluenza," worn down by the pursuit of high status. Parody display items project an attitude of, "I'm here to kick back and enjoy life." The retailer addresses this one by creating a shopping context of fun.

Researchers at New York University and Israel Institute of Technology[101] saw another motivation for shoppers slumming in their product choices: Shame.

In one of their studies, college students were more interested in learning about a T-shirt tattooed with a sophisticated design when the T-shirt was worn by a grocery store packer than when worn by a fellow college student. In another of the researchers' studies, students developed a higher likelihood of buying a wireless charger when they saw it used by a security guard than by a college student.

The irony here is that the attraction to the product depends on aspirational drives. Who was using the wireless charger made a difference only if the college student study participant considered technological innovativeness to be important.

However, the fundamental reason for parody display is the consumer's desire to be distinctive. Everyone else is wearing the aspirational wardrobe. "I'll create a striking image by incorporating merchandise, services, experiences, and beliefs others don't expect," these shoppers say. The retailer leverages this motivation via contrast in marketing and merchandising. Show the lower-class entity surrounded by the usual aspirational things. This contrasts with the "secret handshake" basis for distinctiveness I discussed in Chapter 2, in which consumers who belong to a group seek subtle cues for public display.

People who want to belong to a group may conform to the group's preferences, but the underlying desire for personalization remains. This extends to the shopper's personal history. When people are feeling lonely, they become interested in items which remind them of their personal history in years gone by. In studies at Arizona State University and Erasmus University,[102] this included preferences regarding automobiles, food brands, TV shows, movies, and even shower soap. At another point in the research, people who had been dropped from a game were offered a cookie carrying a brand name popular in the person's past. Those who ate the treat ended up complaining less of loneliness than they did before. This was less true when the treat did not carry a brand name which was nostalgic for the person.

To be sure, talking with a lonely person is a straightforward way of helping them know they belong—belong in your store shopping, that is. We can identify a passion evidenced by lonely consumers to visit stores where staff greet shoppers by name. We love to hear others say our name, when it's said to welcome us. That's retailer personalization.

Some shoppers carry a self-image of stability regarding how they assess products and services for purchase. They view themselves as using similar criteria and as probably making the same choices again in the future if the circumstances are similar. Compared to shoppers with a self-image of low stability, the shoppers with high-stability self-images appreciate personalized recommendations more and are more receptive to learning from the salesperson.

How do we change self-images of low stability into self-images of high stability in order to increase our influence? Ask questions that include the word "you." These set up the shopper to describe the criteria they employ in making purchase decisions and recall the instances in which they've used those criteria:

"In the past, what standards have you used in selecting a floral arrangement? How did those standards work out for you in a few instances you remember?"

Involving your customer in the production of the product they're purchasing can satisfy the desire for personalization. Researchers at Norwegian School of Economics[103] found that when consumers prepared a meal themselves rather than having it prepared for them, the positive evaluations both of the meal and the raw ingredients climbed. Not only that, but the consumers' reports of the degree of saltiness and spiciness they preferred in a meal changed toward whatever the level of saltiness and spiciness were in the meal they had prepared. These consumers were giving themselves reasons to savor, or at least tolerate, whatever they'd created.

A related stream of findings is from what I call the "mirror studies," yet another echo of the "marketing to the mirror" theme. Placing a mirror behind the counters where you accept complaints reduces the intensity of customers' extreme dissatisfaction. This finding by researchers at Bayer Healthcare, Columbia University, and Maastricht University[104] deserves an explanation: When a consumer sees an image of herself, her self-awareness increases. This leads to the consumer subconsciously considering what part she played in causing the unsatisfactory experience.

Mirrors catch us so we'll pause and look at ourselves. The reflection in the mirror leads the consumer to sense the extreme quality of the emotions they're experiencing, arousing the sort of self-accountability that eases the irritation.

A video camera attached to a monitor, both of which are easily spotted by the consumer, accomplishes the same result. Having just the camera by itself helps, although it's not as effective as the full setup.

Did I hear you say the placement of a large mirror won't work out for you, and you're concerned consumers won't notice the video camera? Then use psychological mirrors. Some consumer scientists have suggested asking the consumer questions which include words like "you" and "your," the same research-based tactic for changing self-images of low stability into self-images of high stability. Other researchers have recommended using words like "I," "my," and "mine" on signage in the area.

The effect occurs when the customer is asked or asks herself to evaluate the shopping trip or the experience with the product. It does not occur at the time of the experience itself. That's why the mirror at the complaint desk works in this way.

The effect reduces the intensity of extreme positive emotions as well. After looking at themselves in a mirror, customers are more likely to take credit for their part in highly pleasant shopping experiences, reducing the credit given to the retailer.

The effect makes extreme emotions more moderate. Therefore, it works best for you with people who are so upset it becomes difficult to resolve the complaint. When a mildly disappointed customer looks at himself in the mirror, it can instead increase the intensity of the negative emotion.

Also, the effect occurs only when there is a plausible reason for the consumer to conclude they might have partial responsibility for an unsatisfactory experience, such as a failure to follow usage instructions.

Over the history of retailing, mirrors in stores have been recommended as a way to add light and dilute the perception of crowding. It turns out that this also holds true in lightening up and diluting intense dissatisfaction.

The lessons for retailers from research findings such as these are to use mirrors strategically and to invite shoppers to participate in the design of products they buy and the delivery of services they purchase. The product or service will then be more likely to reflect the characteristics of the consumer.

Present the coproduction offer as an invitation to the shopper, not as a requirement. Many consumers prefer to purchase turnkey solutions, with the retailer taking full responsibility for production decisions. There are plenty of diners who appreciate a restaurant meal much more than their home-cooked ones.

Personalized coproduction does increase "the endowment effect," consumer psychologists' term for how people set a higher value on objects they own than on equivalent objects they do not. Among other behaviors, the endowment effect helps explain why people hesitate tossing a salad with an expiration date from last week when they wouldn't eat at a friend's house a salad with identical ingredients if the expiration date had passed. The endowment effect also explains why people resist trading in used items with you at a price you find attractive. The hesitations are greater with customized items and items the consumer has used.

Findings from a set of five research studies at Boston University and University of Pittsburgh[105] suggest you mobilize empathy to ease disagreements due to the endowment effect. When you empathize with the consumer who is wanting to sell you an item and acknowledge the special value the item has to them, you've set the groundwork for fruitful negotiations. The researchers saw the endowment effect result in differences of over 20% between price estimates of buyers and sellers of used merchandise, and then saw these differences reduced significantly when the buyer evidenced empathy.

A University of Toronto[106] study finds that if the shopper has their mate, partner, or children with them, the endowment effect is stronger than if the shopper is unaccompanied when dealing with a potential purchaser. The shopper will hold out for a higher trade-in price. This might be because it's easier to establish mutual empathy one-to-one. If the person does have family or friends along and you sense the endowment effect arising, see if you can convince the person to go to a separate area for your negotiations. Failing this, find similarities between this consumer's situation with family and friends and your own, then talk about those for a little while.

Some consumers, by the nature of their skills and personality, are good at connecting with others. These consumers evidence less of the endowment effect when in negotiations regarding the sale of their merchandise to retailers. If you, as a retailer, have regulars who sell you items for resale or trade-in, reach out to those of the regulars who show this ability to connect with you. For a consignment retailer, those clients who bring items and describe the type of person who would get the most from the items are those clients who are especially likely to set realistic prices free of the endowment effect.

Any shopper asking for personalization is asking to feel special. That's why it works to personalize not only dealing, but also deals.

"Thank you for coming to my store and making this purchase. Before you leave, one more thing. I might be able to offer you an unusually good deal on the insulated travel mug pictured here. The mug usually sells for $15. I was able to get a very limited quantity of them to sell for $5. If you might be interested, I'll ask you to take one of the slips of paper from this bowl and open the paper. If it has a star on it, I'll give you a certificate you can use to buy one mug for $5 when the mugs arrive a week from today."

That's roughly the offer made by Santa Clara University[107] researchers to two groups of consumers. What distinguished the two groups was the number of paper slips in the bowl. It was either six slips or two.

What the consumers were not told is that every single piece of paper had a star on it. Everybody came out a winner.

Did the number of slips make a difference in purchase behavior?

There was no statistically significant difference in the percentage of consumers in each group who said they'd be interested in drawing out a slip of paper. But there was a big difference in how many came back to actually make the purchase. Of those who thought they'd picked a winning slip from two, about 4% returned to claim the discount. For those in the six-slip condition, about 27% returned, ready to buy.

The researchers attribute the difference to degree of distinctiveness. Feeling exclusive, lucky, and grateful impels buying.

When you tell a customer they're receiving a price discount, they'll build good will toward your store. If you add that the discount isn't available to every other customer, the good will might be even greater.

Realize that your announcement also could make the customer uncomfortable. Be consistent in your policies and be ready to explain the reason for the discount. Otherwise, the customer can get angry, thinking that your store pricing is highly arbitrary or even discriminatory. In accord with a personalization appeal, attribute the discounts to demographics ("A 15% discount to senior citizens.") or marketing measures ("A 15% discount to first-time purchasers." "A 15% discount on purchases before 10 AM."). If you've reason to believe the shopper is superstitious, of the sort discussed in the prior chapter, add luck to the mix ("You're lucky to be a senior citizen so you get this discount." "You came in the store at the lucky time for a special discount.")

The multitude of available data analysis techniques allows even small retail businesses to personalize discount coupons. By keeping track of what the customer has bought—and perhaps even what the shopper has considered, but not bought—you develop a profile and then offer that individual what the profile suggests would carry special appeal.

The draw of such customized discounts occurs even if the person doesn't use the coupons. In fact, in a University of Virginia[108] study, mere exposure to a coupon campaign had a bigger impact on store sales figures than did the frequency of coupon redemption. Recipients who did not redeem their coupons accounted for about 60% of the additional amounts spent on items—both items which were promoted and items not promoted by the coupons. Discount coupons create for all recipients an image of the issuing store as wanting to save shoppers money. This leads to more store visits and a greater interest in making purchases at the store. The higher relative impact on non-redeemers comes about because with most coupon campaigns, only a small percentage of recipients will make use of the coupon offer.

This is true for store customers overall, whether or not the coupon offers are personalized. Customers are especially likely to notice and to remember when the items you've discounted on the coupon are of primary interest to them. In turn, discounts which are noticed will cultivate a customer's impression that all prices at your store offer good value. Personalized discounts communicate caring about the individual.

Another angle in delivering rewards is to give a treat to an excellent customer in the presence of others. When delivered in front of an entourage, the nature of the reward can produce equal customer gratitude even if the reward is otherwise less impressive—such as a lower-cost gift. Or if the reward is large enough for the customer to share it with the entourage, that is an even more positive experience for the customer.

The entourage can consist of friends and/or family. It is the shopper's desire to impress those others which characterizes an entourage. A desire to impress also affects what the shopper will choose to purchase in the presence of the entourage.

This last finding means a shopper whose preferences you think you know well can make quite different choices when coming in with a different group of people. For instance, when shopping with family members along, a consumer is more likely to take financial risks in purchases than when shopping with a group of friends. But the shopper with family is less likely to select highly unusual products or services.

It can be frustrating for the conscientious salesperson. You and your staff are priding yourselves on knowing what each customer likes as soon as they walk through the door, and you find that your assumption was wrong this time. The way to get back on track with your mindreading is to start pairing the shopper's preferences with the characteristics of the entourage. A bonus benefit is that you can then sell well to the entourage members, too. Related to this, your odds are greater of selling well to the shopper who comes back later to buy a gift for a member of their entourage.

When selecting a gift, personalization requires the shopper to think in depth about the recipient and so enables presentation of the gift in an especially meaningful way. This dynamic holds true for more than adults. People like to personalize for the children and pets they love.

At the same time, personalization demands knowledge of what alternatives are available and of the tradeoffs. The shopper may ask you for help. How much direction should you provide?

The research-based answer: Limit the design support.

The more time and mental effort the gift giver devotes to the personalizing, the more they are willing to pay for the item. This is because a shopper places value on their time and effort. Answer the shopper's questions, but if asked, "What should I pick?," respond as a first answer, "Well, you know the recipient better than I do."

Suggest to the shopper brands that carry a less dominant product personality. When trying to personalize strong brands, the gift shopper often feels a need to share credit with the brand's design staff for the outcome. They'll end up less pleased with their personalization.

Provide many ways to personalize. Offer gift wrapping as a value-added service. Show a variety of tags or greeting cards from which the shopper can select. If the shopper wants to buy a gift card, help them personalize that. Individualize your gift cards and holders with a selection of themes—such as sports and travel—a range of colors, and enough space to write a message to the recipient.

In all of your approaches to personalizing for the shopper, pay attention to changes. Each time one of your regular customers comes in, do you and your staff notice what's new with the customer that you could take into account in selling well? If you think the person would like you to notice the changes, do you comment on them? If the customer doesn't show you or tell you about changes, do you ask when appropriate? Do you make a mental note about changes soon after the customer arrives at your store so that you'll remember the changes better?

The same bank is held up by the same robber five weeks in a row. The same police officer interviews the bank staff after the robbery each of the days. Arriving this fifth time, the officer says to the staff, "Look, at this point, I've gotten a really thorough description of the guy. I've talked to you four times already. But on the off chance you've something to add, I'll ask if there is anything more you can tell me about what this robber looks like."

"Hmmm," says one of the tellers, "I have noticed that each time he comes in now, he's a little better dressed than the last time."

RIMinders

- When purchasing used items from a consumer, acknowledge any special value the item has had for them and negotiate with the shopper away from the shopper's family.
- In assessing the effectiveness of couponing campaigns, look at the differences in total store sales, not only at differences in items for which the coupon gave a discount.
- If asked by a gift shopper for help in selecting an item, make your first reply, "Well, you know the recipient better than I do."
- Offer the goal-seeker a broad variety of assistance items at the start and then, as the customer feels closer to achieving the goal, offer a more limited selection.
- Be prepared to satisfy desires for both conformity and distinctiveness within the same shopper: Conformity with groups the shopper belongs to or aspires to belong to. Distinctiveness from groups the shopper does not want to be associated with.
- Place special emphasis on allowing a shopper to personalize their choices when the shopper has exerted effort in making the purchase, is a senior citizen, is purchasing a fashion item or trendy item, or is shopping with a group that is showing high conformity in their choices.
- Involving your customer in the production of the product they're purchasing can satisfy the desire for personalization. Present the coproduction offer as an invitation to the shopper, not as a requirement. Many consumers prefer to purchase turnkey solutions, with the retailer taking full responsibility for production decisions.
- To build a desire for distinctiveness, ask, "What about this product do you like that your friends would also like?" To encourage conformity, ask, "What about this product do your friends like and you also like?"

- To gather information helpful in personalizing offerings, provide the shopper adequate privacy when answering your questions; give a few instances of sensitive information other shoppers have shared with you; ensure the shopper appreciates how answering the intrusive questions will be helpful to them; ask permission to ask the intrusive questions; and remember the answers the shopper gives you.
- To strengthen the association between a shopper's characteristics and their choice of products, have mirrors in the shopping area and use words like "you" in talking with the shopper.
- Personalize discount offers as well as merchandise selections.
- Recognize that offering even minor variations can be enough to ease a shopper's insistence on customization. This is especially true when you provide the shopper many ways to personalize.

10

A Merchant Mindset

⁓

Selling well requires more than an aroused awareness of the often overlooked shopper motivations I've discussed for you so far. Selling well also requires you to have a merchant mindset and customer-focused staffing.

As a fundamental, all store personnel should honor salesmanship.

Going as far back as Homer's *The Odyssey*, retailers have been depicted as slimy and well beneath the station of those who manufacture the products sold. Says Euryalus to Odysseus, "Art thou such a one as comes and goes in a benched ship, a master of sailors that are merchantmen, one with a memory for his freight, or that hath the charge of a cargo homeward bound, and of greedily gotten gains? Thou seemest not a man of thy hands!"

In today's computer-generated word clouds, "selling" has stronger associations with "tricking" than with "serving." In the public's thoughts, the central objective of salesmanship training is how to grab the legs of each passerby, yank them upside down, and shake hard enough to dislodge from pockets and purses every last penny and all available credit cards.

Those perceptions are not without justification. Many retailers do forget to keep their skills sharp and do neglect to deliver full value to the shopper. These less-than-honorable merchants probe with questions which put consumers on the defensive, polluting the well for other merchants.

They fail to use questions properly in order to clarify shopper needs and desires the shopper may not have recognized.

Please stop for a moment now and bring to mind the retailers you respect. Use your talents at getting answers to ask yourself what distinguishes these individuals. Honor them, honor the best in yourself as a retailer, and honor salesmanship.

Odysseus knew to honor the courage necessary for selling and the ability of merchants to impress others. Homer writes that, in response to Euryalus' taunt, Odysseus looked fiercely at him and then, "leaped to his feet, and caught up a weight larger than the rest, a huge weight heavier far than those wherewith the Phaeacians contended in casting. With one whirl he sent it from his stout hand, and the stone flew hurtling. And the Phaeacians, of the long oars, those mariners renowned, crouched to earth beneath the rushing of the stone. Beyond all the marks it flew, so lightly it sped from his hand. And Athene in the fashion of a man marked the place, and spake and hailed him."

In today's litigious environment, throwing stones toward consumers who question your intentions would inflate your business liability insurance premiums unacceptably. But decisively demonstrating to suspicious customers your retailing professionalism is a great idea.

Next, let's add educated optimism and justified perseverance to the mix, using another fable. It is said that when Robert Fulton first demonstrated his steamboat, a man standing on the banks kept yelling loudly, "He won't be able to start 'er." Then as the steamboat did move with increasing certainty, the heckler stood silent, a shocked look on his face. Moments later, though, he yelled again. "He won't be able to stop 'er."

This anecdote comes to my mind occasionally as I go about my work implementing retail profitability initiatives. Producing the best results from these projects involves more than training and consulting. Direction comes from focus groups, surveys, and other assessments of the retailing neighborhood's strengths, challenges, and opportunities.

Often, what makes the difference between a successful initiative and a less successful one is the ability of the neighboring retailers to collaborate. And it takes no more than one heckler to hijack the collaboration. The heckler asks perfectly reasonable questions about the profitability tactics—questions which stimulate thinking by the others. So far, quite good.

But then there is no end to the probes and the doubts. Soon, the heckler is not moving the discussion forward, but instead freezing it in place. A voice of caution becomes a force of obstruction.

When this happens, the organizational dynamics don't stop there. Merchants are, after all, action-oriented. In the retail profitability initiatives I'm coordinating, I've seen how others in the group meetings react to the heckler's obstructionism by lurching forward prematurely, pushing for action without full consideration of what the retailers will be getting themselves into.

Early versions of Robert Fulton and Robert R. Livingston's steamboat did have difficulty progressing up the river because the designers had not sufficiently accounted for resistance from the water. During an August 8, 1803 trial, the boat sank. Even at its best four years later in New York State, steamboat travel was deliberate, but slow.

In your own retail profitability initiatives involving collaboration among merchants or among your own store's team members, steam on through to success. Think deliberatively. Also keep in mind that if you waste enough time looking, you can always find something to complain about. You won't be able to start 'er or stop 'er in sufficiently profitable ways.

Successful merchants realize that in the fast-changing reality of retailing, those who stand still are sure to be left behind. Their operating principle is often "Ready. Fire. Aim." rather than "Ready. Aim. Fire." They are "Give it a try and see what happens" people.

Still, act from purpose, not panic. "Don't just stand there, do something," or some version of it, has been shouted at one time or another by every manager throughout history. But there's the converse to consider: "Don't just do something, stand there," has been publically proclaimed by a wide range of well-known individuals, from 1960's radical Abbie Hoffman to U.S. President Ronald Reagan to the White Rabbit in the Disney version of "Alice in Wonderland." In addition to freezing us into destructive inaction, panic can cause premature action. Instead of thinking through the alternatives and selecting the least bad choice, the retailer moves too soon.

Fear can confuse a retailer, preventing them from taking actions necessary to stay on top of events. Fear can shut down the creative thinking needed to navigate through setbacks. On the other hand, fear also can help you move fast and think sharply. The trick is to keep the fear manageable. A century ago, psychologists Robert M. Yerkes and John Dillingham Dodson sketched out what became known as the Yerkes-Dodson Law. In terms of retailing management and fear, the law becomes "As fear builds in a retailer, the quality of their thinking and the effectiveness of their actions improves. To a point. Beyond that point, as fear builds further, the quality of the retailer's thinking and actions drops fast." If your fear seems to be getting too high, switch to a less demanding retailing task briefly. Research indicates that success there causes the fear to decrease.

To best utilize the energy which fear provides, distinguish activity from accomplishment.

When I was a psychology doctoral student at Stanford, I suffered from SDS. The place was riddled with the malady, and still is, so I figure I contracted it from other students. SDS is Stanford Duck Syndrome, a well-known phenomenon on campus in which students seem cheerful, but all the while are furiously paddling their legs to stay afloat.

Every fine university has its version of SDS. So does every successful retail store.

The closest to a cure for SDS is to consistently keep in mind that activity is related to accomplishment, but they are not the same. Furious paddling might energize you and, through serendipity, bring success. However, you're most likely to be propelled toward profitability when you've decided where you want to go and aim there. Moreover, excessive activity fatigues you.

You'll want key performance indicators to measure your progress along the way. Increased store footsteps can increase store revenues, so measure store footsteps. But don't confuse store footsteps with store revenues. It's helpful to stay busy in order to keep shelves fully faced, but not when that impedes you fully facing the shopper who's just walked up with a question. In this case, a break from the activity allows for the important accomplishment.

"What gets measured gets done" is a helpful epigram for retailers. But a big difficulty is that monitoring requires focusing on the here-and-now, and the here-and-now includes all the incoming demands on our resources. Paying the pressing bills by the due date, ordering up inventory in time for prompt delivery, resolving the argument between employees before things get really ugly. This pulls our thinking away from the longer-term perspective.

There's also something else: The psychological research says that when a retailer carefully monitors results toward achieving long-term goals they've set, one consequence is that time seems to pass more slowly. And that, in turn, makes the goal seem more distant. Ironically, then, monitoring our achievements so far can actually interfere with what gets measured ending up getting done.

A hint about how to unscramble this riddle comes from a classic study which itself produced another puzzling riddle: In an article titled "Obesity, Food Deprivation, and Supermarket Shopping Behavior," which appeared in the *Journal of Personality and Social Psychology* more than 45 years ago, R.E. Nisbett and D.E. Kanouse reported something quite surprising: People on a diet buy less when they are hungry than when they have eaten recently.

It certainly would seem that hungry dieters would buy more, not less. What's going on? The answer is that the hunger became a reminder to the dieters that they were in the process of making real progress. They could sense how far they'd come toward the payoff of taking it off.

The hint for you: Avoid continuous monitoring of how far you need to go to achieve long-term, somewhat fuzzy goals. Instead, regularly monitor how far you've already progressed toward each clearly defined business objective.

Start with small steps using resources at hand or within easy reach before taking large steps which require stretching to acquire substantial new resources. Until you've achieved experience and momentum, aim for quick, inexpensive, incremental improvements rather than transformational change. One reason for this is that if you depend on many other people for project implementation, chances are some of those people will aim to impede your success. Those kinds of people lurk everywhere in the world of business.

Retailing requires human interactions, and a universal component of human interactions is resistance. For every retail seller, there are buyers and regulators. Buyers fight back against feelings they're relinquishing free will. Regulators, beyond being expected to legitimately protect society's interests, want to feel important. They want their expertise and influence to be acknowledged. When it isn't, they push back against you even harder.

The merchant mindset favors persuasion and negotiation over manipulation and coercion. When using powerful psychological techniques to create the future for you, your staff, your shoppers, and the other stakeholders in the success of your business, proceed patiently. The Chapter 5 discussion of priming documents the power in planting the seed early so it has time to grow. For instance, when shoppers might resist purchasing a product because of its country of origin, research findings indicate those resistances are less when country of origin information is presented in advance.

Celebrate and publicize achievements along the way. These are opportunities to recruit additional resources. But cultivate a merchant mindset, which steers clear of perfectionism.

On a "Late Show With David Letterman," actor Peter O'Toole revealed how the dry cleaner shop he used inspired his choice of an epitaph. A leather jacket he sent to that cleaners came back with a note attached: "It distresses us to return work which is not perfect."

"I'm having that on my tombstone," Mr. O'Toole announced.

Perfection may be a noble aim for a retailer, but it also may expedite use of tombstones. One for the business and one for the businessperson.

Keep your eye on many important tasks at once. But allow some tasks to be in your peripheral vision. The central focus should be on tactics and measures that, if they fall too far short, substantially impact your profitability.

The successful merchant engages in skillful selective neglect. You can do it all. The problem is you can't do it all at the same time. There are many ways to improve your profitability as a retailer. You almost certainly don't have the resources to implement them all simultaneously. And more, it turns out, is not always better.

Researchers at University of Mannheim in Germany and University of Texas-Austin[109] found that customers who are adequately satisfied are willing to pay higher prices than are customers who are barely satisfied. But the researchers also found that developing customer willingness to pay yet higher prices generally requires ensuring those customers are consistently very highly satisfied. The costs of doing this might make it unprofitable. If so, why not be satisfied with adequate customer satisfaction?

Researchers at Duke University and University of California-Berkeley[110] find that advertising a warranty has no effect on consumer perceptions of retailer and product quality unless both retailer reputation and manufacturer reputation are in other ways flawlessly positive. So until you're confident that your shoppers absolutely revere your reputation, why advertise warranties?

Satisfice. Studies at Swarthmore College, University of Pennsylvania, University of California-Riverside, and University of British Columbia[111] concluded that satisficers have higher life satisfaction, happiness, optimism, and self-esteem than do people who hold out for perfection. Accept less-than-perfect alternatives so you can move on to the next ideas you want to implement.

Moving on to those next ideas while refining your current ideas is crucial because you might want to be a portfolio entrepreneur instead of a serial entrepreneur. Portfolio entrepreneurs are those business people who diversify in their retailing endeavors, running a set of businesses at the same time. Serial entrepreneurs pursue a single business at a time.

Researchers at Warwick Business School, Durham Business School, and Nottingham University[112] compared the fortunes of serial entrepreneurs to those of portfolio entrepreneurs. They discovered important differences between successful and unsuccessful serial entrepreneurs. When the successful serial entrepreneurs had positive results, they moved quickly to build on those results. Because they focused on the one business concept, they could recognize successful results promptly and then devote all their resources to carrying out the next steps in their plan.

Their close attention to the one business concept at a time helped them see trends and thereby not only predict the likely future of their retail business, but also plan for how to create the future they desire for their retail business.

They were, on the whole, not discouraged by failures. Unanticipated obstacles were seen as learning opportunities, and prolonged setbacks motivated a search for better alternatives. Those alternatives might include abandoning the current enterprise and promptly moving on to the next entrepreneurial challenge. Successful serial entrepreneurs knew when to cut their losses.

So why did the researchers go on to recommend that a merchant be a portfolio entrepreneur instead? Because many serial entrepreneurs are not successful. They fail to spot when to cut their losses.

Compared to serial entrepreneurs, portfolio entrepreneurs generally learn better from failure because they have less investment in defending their prior actions. Their pride isn't tied so tightly to one enterprise. They experience less pain from the failure.

Associated with this, serial entrepreneurs are less likely than portfolio entrepreneurs to see accurately what they themselves did wrong. Their zeal to move on could result in serial failures.

Taken together, these sets of research findings point out the tradeoffs for you, the merchant, in focusing on a single business at a time. Even within one small to midsize store, the owner/operator must carry out a broad range of duties. Taking on more than one business could quickly corrode effectiveness in any of them. Still, beware of overinvestment in the one business to the point where the pain of admitting failure prevents you from promptly taking advisable corrective actions.

Whichever kind of entrepreneur you are, unambiguously state how much you're willing to lose before you'll pull the plug on an initiative. Agree with yourself that you might change this limit, but require yourself to temporarily retreat from the project for a careful assessment before making any such change. Keep your promises to yourself and to others optimistic, while at the same time realistic.

As you're moving along the open road, look straight ahead most of the time. However, also anticipate danger, scanning for risks approaching from unexpected directions so that you can take evasive action. Go beyond predicting your future. Create your future. Don't trap yourself by waiting for the marketplace or the broader economy to force you into reacting. Instead, do your best job of predicting what the government, regulatory agencies, your retailing competition, and your shoppers are likely to do. Then consult your predictions to grab the initiative.

And as a vital part of creating your future, learn from the past. Don't dwell on the past, though. That would discourage you, and recall that successful retailers are optimistic. Creating your future does generate optimism. It's a particular kind of optimism. It's not a belief that everything will turn out fine, no matter what. Instead, it's a conviction that you are capable of using the strengths of your business to achieve high profitability.

Like a lack of optimism and a fear of the future, excessive anger about the past disrupts our business focus. In a 1911 story, "Gertrude the Governess," Canadian humorist Stephen Leacock, wrote, "Lord Ronald said nothing; he flung himself from the room, flung himself upon his horse, and rode madly off in all directions." Don't be a Lord Ronald.

During April 2013, Stanford University held a "Compassion & Business Conference" at which Jay Narayanan from National University of Singapore shared a tale to illustrate the value of forgiveness: A group of people were asked to estimate the degree of steepness of a hill. Before giving the estimate, some of the people had been instructed to think about grudges they carry with them. The other people had been instructed to remember in detail a time each had chosen to forgive someone who had committed a significant mistake.

Prof. Narayanan reported that the grudge holders judged the same hill as steeper than did the forgivers. Compassion smoothed out the journey, it seemed.

I agree with that insight. Over the years, I've found that it consumes loads of mental energy when trying to remember who I'm supposed to be mad at. I'd rather devote the energy to surmounting retail business challenges.

I'm no sucker, though. I also support the saying "Trick me once, shame on you. Trick me twice, shame on me." Learn from the past without all the emotions of revenge.

Also getting in the way of any merchant's open roads is the reality that there's already too much data for us to comfortably analyze, and more data keeps popping up. We can succumb to information overload as much as can our shoppers. To make good decisions, know what's going on while avoiding analysis paralysis. Start with the big picture and select where to drill down for details. You want to decide what products to purchase for your store, what services to develop, how to advertise and publicize, what to prune out of your merchandising mix. All these require attention to where the marketplace is going, not only how things are now. Skim the data. Get an overview.

At the same time, there will be areas where you need the details. What specific types of consumers are purchasing which products? Which suppliers are providing the best package for your situation, when you consider point-of-purchase materials and staff training in addition to wholesale price?

The sell-well merchant mindset slices and dices in order to identify opportunities for improving profitability. For instance, instead of looking at consumer survey results for all respondents together, you might pull out the results for all respondents who report a household income greater than $100,000 and say they are grandmothers interested in giving your product to a girl under the age of 5.

To do such segmentation, you'll need to think out in advance what criteria you might be using. If you didn't ask the survey respondents for household income, grandparent status, or age and gender of intended gift recipients, you won't be able to segment the results for the example I used.

Among the many possibilities:

- **Lifestyle profiles.** What beliefs, feelings, and intentions distinguish those who shop at your store frequently from those who do not?
- **Store-specific profiles.** What distinguishes people who shop at your store instead of, or in addition to, shopping at other specific stores?
- **Offering-specific profiles.** What characterizes the shoppers for the different sorts of products and services your store offers?
- **Demographic profiles.** What can you learn from the survey that will help you customize your marketing and selling? What are the differences between your female and male target audiences? The Millennials from the Baby Boomers? The bilinguals from the monolinguals?

The psychographic division most thoroughly supported by consumer psychology research is into promotion-focused—consisting of shoppers looking to enhance their current situation—and prevention-focused—consisting of shopper wanting to avoid losses. Another popular grouping is into mission shoppers—who burst into your aisles looking for a specific item or for advice on solving a specific problem—and possibilities shoppers—who stroll the store considering what they might buy now or maybe during a future visit.

Whatever categories you use should reflect genuine differences important in you improving your profitability. How to determine that? A sophisticated statistical technique called "cluster analysis" and its equally sophisticated cousin, named "discriminant analysis" can accomplish this when used by experts working in collaboration with you. Applied to a matrix of customer response measures—such as item selection, point-of-sale data, and questionnaire answers—cluster analysis and discriminant analysis can help you identify the best groupings.

Proper use of sophisticated statistics, such as in cluster analysis and discriminant analysis, is one data-driven technique requiring the use of expert consultants. The other is in conducting depth-oriented focus groups and deriving the results.

Depth-oriented focus groups aim to identify consumers' secret motivations by climbing deep into the subconscious minds of the group members. Depth-oriented focus groups can provide merchants with a compelling retailer's edge.

In my opinion, conducting these groups properly requires competence in clinical psychology as well as consumer psychology. Among other things, I've occasionally seen instances where digging into the subconscious requires followup emotional decompression before sending a focus group participant back into the night.

Even if you agree with my opinion, you'll still need enough expertise to oversee the focus group facilitator. My primary advice parallels what I say about other tasks for which you hire an outsider because of their technical expertise and what I said in Chapter 6 about a healthy skepticism toward research results: When the conclusions from a project don't make good sense to you based on your experiences as a retailer, start out by asking yourself if you might have misunderstood what the consultant said or you might have been blind to factors the consultant discovered.

The most valuable conclusions from retail consultants lead to you saying, "Yes, now I see what I hadn't recognized before." If you decide you did understand the consultant correctly, you weren't blind to important factors, and yet the conclusions don't ring true, then consider what the consultant is telling you as having a high nonsense potential.

With depth-oriented focus groups, an error I've sometimes noticed is a failure to attend to the participants' purchase intentions. So much attention is devoted to the emotional drivers and the subconscious beliefs that the facilitator overlooks the payoff theme: What will our target audiences end up buying, how much of their resources are they willing to spend, and where will they end up making their purchases?

Beliefs will be assessed beginning with probes such as, "To what degree do their sales staff want to get you the right product for your needs?" Feelings will be assessed starting with probes like, "When you buy a product there, how confident are you that you've made a good decision?" But as you're watching the video of the focus group, do you see the prelude to the money shot with a probe like, "Next time you need a product carried by that store, how likely are you to shop there?"

Those probes are at the surface. Each determines what you'll dig into. For your business to reach its full potential, be sure that your consultant is exploring all three areas when conducting a depth-oriented focus group. Know your potential customers' beliefs and feelings, and their intentions.

Again, the theme is to always view data collection results through your lens as a knowledgeable merchant.

Ready to give that theme a try? Okay, then please critique the following:

Ryerson University[113] researchers developed a mathematical model to assess the ongoing effectiveness of customer loyalty programs—sometimes called frequent shopper programs—which reward customers for their continuing business. Many retailers feel that well-designed loyalty programs motivate customers to keep coming back. The Ryerson researchers believed their mathematical model would test the accuracy of these feelings and indicate how to maximize the monetary return from loyalty programs.

To generate data for the mathematical model, it was assumed that loyalty program members who purchased an item were given a coupon for a 15% discount on a subsequent purchase to be made within two months.

I see these as acceptable assumptions, since prior research has shown that the loyalty program reward most popular with customers is a percentage discount on future purchases of items selected by the customer, and a 15% discount is at least close to sufficient to motivate a shopper, although Weber's Law, which I described in Chapter 6, would predicate a 20% discount.

The resulting mathematical model reflected how loyalty programs do indeed influence consumers to become repeat customers. Then further analysis showed how once the habit is developed, there is no evidence of further gain from continuing the loyalty program. In fact, the model indicated that, in order to compensate for the revenue lost from the 15% discount, it would be necessary to raise the price on that item or on other merchandise.

Therefore, concluded the Ryerson researchers, you should discontinue the loyalty program once you've established the initial habit.

The consumer behavior study was carefully done. But the recommendations to the retailer don't make sense to me. Can you figure out why I say that?

Well, in my opinion, there are two flaws:

- If the program is effective, the retailer should continue using it to build loyalty in more shoppers, including those coming into the store after the program began.
- A frequent shopper program has objectives other than building a general tendency to return. Principally, it also allows you to track each customer's purchase history in ways you can use to target sales promotions.

The mathematical model was overly limited in scope. It didn't match real retailing life. Maybe I should have spotted that immediately when I saw that the article about the research was published not in a retailing or marketing journal, but in *Computers & Industrial Engineering*.

For another example of the need to interpret through a merchant mindset, consider a study which concluded that the higher the degree of customer satisfaction with a store, the lower the share that store has of the marketplace's expenditures. It would seem that to grow revenues, the retailer should aim for low customer satisfaction.

The study report, by Lopo L. Rego, Neil A. Morgan, and Claes Fornell was published in the September 2013 issue of *Journal of Marketing*. What distinguishes this study is the breadth of U.S. consumer markets they included and the long time period covered by the data they analyzed. Both these factors make the conclusions of the study more believable.

Here's my interpretation of those conclusions:

- When a store has a high share of the market, that store becomes less likely to continue to give excellent customer service. This might be because the retail business is struggling to keep up with all the traffic they're handling. It might be because they figure they no longer need to dazzle the customers.

- Over the full range of customer satisfaction levels—from very low to very high—customer satisfaction is not closely correlated—either negatively or positively—with gaining market share. This is in accord with the University of Mannheim/University of Texas findings about customer satisfaction I presented earlier in this chapter. When these findings are put together with the one about stores with high market share not continuing to give excellent customer service, it explains why statistical analyses show that the higher the degree of customer satisfaction with a store, the lower the share that store has of the customer's expenditures.

- However, there's an exception to this: When a store's customer satisfaction score is significantly higher than that of other stores easily available to the shoppers, then market share does usually grow. Because continuing to maintain outstanding customer service costs money, the path to high net profitability is to give outstanding service only to the degree that you separate yourself from the competition. This conclusion puts a refined spin on those University of Mannheim/University of Texas findings.

Whenever someone suggests a profitability tactic to you, take care that they're not basing the suggestion on an unrealistically limited perspective:

- **Better or worse than what?** Set a baseline. Before implementing a tactic, measure how things are now. How many units did you sell last month, when you hadn't started the intervention? How many units did you sell for the first month after the intervention was fully and competently implemented?

- **Measure twice and cut once.** To the carpenter, this proverb means to double-check for accuracy before sawing the piece of wood. To the retailer trying out a technique, I suggest you take the proverb to mean, "Measure for success or failure in multiple ways." Maybe the technique didn't produce a noticeable difference in average purchase size, but there was an important boost to repeat business.

- **In what ways is it working, and how well is it working in each of those ways?** The answers are more fruitful than the answer to, "Is it working?," which is too simplistic. You'll maximize profitability by fine-tuning the tactics as you learn from experience and by revising the tactics broadly or even discarding them as you anticipate changes in consumer sentiments. The answers to the more complex questions help you do that by giving you an understanding of the "why," not only the "what."

When analyzing financial indicators, look at the numbers in different ways depending on your objective. For example, consider how you'd figure out the size of your typical retail sale.

Suppose it's been a slow morning with only ten transactions. Two of those were for $100 and eight of them were for $5. The easiest way to calculate the average is to add up the total value and divide by the number of transactions. The total is $240, so the mean average for the ten transactions is $240 divided by ten, or $24. But $24 certainly isn't the typical transaction.

Instead of using only the mean, also look at the mode, the median, and the range. To get the range, look at the lowest and highest values. For the mode, group transaction amounts, such as everything from $0.01-$9.99 into one bucket, $10 to $19.99 into a second bucket, $20 to $29.99 into another bucket, and so on. Then see which bucket has the most entries. In my example, the mode is $0.01-$9.99. To get the median, line up the amounts from highest to lowest and then find the point where half the amounts are below it or equal to it and half the amounts are above it. In my example, the median is $5, and it is the best of the statistics to look at in this case if you want to identify the typical transaction for this slow morning.

Retailers make more money when they aren't deceived by looking at just the mean. Instead, planning is based on conclusions like, "Our typical transaction was $5, the lowest was $5, and the highest was $100."

In surveying shoppers to learn what leads to the typical transaction, begin by detailing your objectives. For instance, do you want to build a business intimacy between your current way of doing business and your shoppers or do you want to gather ideas for improving the way you're currently doing business?

If it's more important to build business intimacy, ask for advice rather than opinions or expectations.

- **Advice** questions are of the form, "What items of advice do you have for our store?"
- **Opinion** items are of the form, "What are your opinions about our store?"
- **Expectations** questions are of the form, "What are your expectations of our store?"

Of the three types, advice questions are the most likely to lead to future purchase intentions by the consumer taking the survey This is because asking for advice gives rise in the consumer to feelings of closeness to the store and a readiness to experience happiness if the store succeeds. In contrast, expectations questions distance the consumer from caring about the fortunes of the store except as a place to satisfy the consumer's self-interested desires.

In other ways, too, the way in which you ask questions of a consumer often affects the likelihood of them giving you more business. Avoid the word "Why?" Shoppers often interpret that question to mean you're challenging the wisdom of their decision. It also challenges the power balance. As I'll touch on in the next chapter with my Outback example, shoppers prefer to believe they have more authority than the retailer in the transaction. Therefore, rather than "why," use softer phrasing such as, "I'm interested in hearing more about what you liked with the item," or "I'd be grateful if you told me more about what you disliked."

If the item you're asking about is one the shopper is evaluating to give pleasure—like a cupcake—having the shopper list the reasons dampens the intensity of the reaction. If the shopper liked the item lots, asking for the explanation makes them like it a bit less. If the shopper truly disliked the item, the recitation of reasons results in the shopper disliking it less. Emotions are experienced holistically. Asking somebody to dissect an emotional reaction decreases the power of the emotion. This is another angle on why having an irate customer look into a mirror reins in the anger, as I discussed in Chapter 9.

Therefore, if a customer is expressing ecstasy about a pleasure-oriented product you've sold them, don't ask too many questions. Second, if a customer is expressing intense dislike, ask them to tell you the reasons and listen carefully. Still, don't have the customer go on for too long. Too much talking will lock into the shopper's mind the bad feelings they're experiencing, and those negative memories make it less likely they'll buy from you in the future.

If the item is primarily utilitarian—such as a bathroom cleanser—the effects of explanation are the opposite of those for a hedonic item. When the shopper explains why they like the item, they come to like it even more. After having explained why they dislike it, they'll dislike it even more. With those negatively-evaluated items, some things are best left unsaid, at least from the retailer's perspective. But there's also a caution on the liking side. Recall that if we ask somebody to dig for reasons they liked an item, they'll run out of things to say and interpret the difficulty to mean, "I guess the item isn't so great after all."

Asking questions of shoppers and then recording what they answer—as is done in consumer survey questionnaires—provides one kind of data. However, the answers you get can be incomplete or misleading. People often don't know why they're doing what they do. As documented throughout Chapter 4 on habits, consumers shop in certain ways for reasons you can discover, but those reasons are often operating at a subconscious level. Even when shoppers know their reasons, they may not want to tell you. It gets even worse when your objective is to predict what your customers and potential customers will be doing next.

Survey respondents often tell a researcher what they think the researcher wants to hear. Recall from Chapter 5 how demand characteristics occur when participants in a study or shoppers in a store believe they've figured out what the experimenter or the retailer is looking for them to do and then mold their behavior to fit. When the consumer believes they've been treated nicely, most will want to help the other person prove a point.

If you have contradictory outcomes after using a profitability tactic, analyze the demand characteristics in the situation. Are some customers trying to meet your expectations, while others are trying to do the opposite of what they think you expect them to do because of reactance?

A way to lessen the bias of demand characteristics in studying consumers is to not just ask them, but also observe and listen to them. Have your sales staff make notes on what they hear shoppers saying to the sales staff and to each other about your products, services, store appearance, and the rest.

Asking customers if you can follow them home probably wouldn't work out well for you in most circumstances. Customers would say no. And if they said yes, the visits would consume your valuable time.

Still, you may have opportunities to visit your customer's home or business locations to install, service, or repair products they've purchased from you. In these cases, observe all you can about how they're using the products.

- What are the uses you didn't expect and can now leverage as selling points to others?
- In what ways, if any, are purchasers misusing the products or not using them to full advantage? How can you improve your instructions when a customer purchases the item?
- What frustrations are users experiencing that could be eased through in-store training or client-site fee-based consultation?
- Which pleasant experiences in the intimacy of your customers' homes can you capture in stories to tell to shoppers and to use in ads with home backdrops?

There are many differences between watching shoppers and quizzing them. The most important one has to do with waste and irritation. If you unobtrusively watch shoppers and end up never employing the findings, you've wasted time and money. But if you ask people to open up their minds and you fail to analyze the results or don't let the respondents know what you're doing differently or why you're not doing anything differently, it's worse than a waste. You've offended the attitude survey respondents, meaning it's less likely they'll open up their minds honestly if you choose to ask them again.

Throughout all of this, the merchant mindset is based on planning your work, then working your plan. In the fast-changing world of retailing, it can be difficult to maintain the discipline to do the second part of this. Iron out that wrinkle by staying sensitive to what gear you are in.

- **Open wounds.** There will be times that unexpected news floods in so fast you must take immediate steps or risk business failure. At these times, you might ask others for ideas and you might consider the tradeoffs in implementation. Still, your primary focus is on short-term bandages. Understandably, you'll deviate from your original plan until the crisis is resolved. Use of your open wounds gear is inevitable, and the deviations from plans are necessary. Still, if you find yourself in open wounds gear as a general business practice, you're not adequately monitoring the environment in which your store functions to spot the opportunities and the threats. Minimize use of this gear.

- **Open minds.** Here's where you welcome all sorts of input, realizing it's always easier to tame down an unrealistic idea than to try to make the same old ideas exciting. This stage calls upon your creativity and teamwork talents. Don't expect yourself to be working your plan here because the plan is not yet fully formed.

- **Open roads.** This is the "work your plan" implementation stage I've referred to throughout this chapter. You cut back on the brainstorming, critically evaluate what you've got, develop your plan based on what's most likely to work for the long-term, and move ahead decisively. It is a stage of determined action. In the open roads stage, the owner/operator of the small to midsize retail business should stay the course. Bind yourself to the task.

In *The Odyssey*, Homer wrote that Odysseus avoided the temptation of the Sirens by having his crew bind him to the mast so that he would not deviate from his intended route when he heard the Sirens' calls. Beyond that, Odysseus ordered his crew to stuff their ears with wax, which they were to keep there until the craft had passed the Sirens' island.

Ensuring that our staff helps us stick to the plan is a good idea. But do recognize there's a danger in preventing all our people and ourselves from sensing distractions which should legitimately lead to us deviating from our previous intentions. The life of a retailer is filled with the unpredictable.

Therefore, along with binding yourself to your plan, provide for regularly monitoring outside developments. That's merchant mindset wisdom, not procrastination or SDS.

RIMinders

- Know the difference between retailing activity and retailing accomplishment.
- Stay aware—and let your coworkers know—whether you are in open minds gear, where you welcome all sorts of input; open roads gear, where you are pursuing a specific plan; or open wounds gear, where you are taking highly directive short-term actions.
- Avoid continuous monitoring of how far you need to go to achieve long-term goals. Instead, regularly monitor how far you've already progressed toward each clearly defined business objective.
- Start with small steps using resources at hand or within easy reach before taking large steps which require stretching to acquire substantial new resources. Plant the seeds for ideas in others and allow time for enthusiasm about the ideas to grow.
- Before gathering data, decide how you'll want to categorize the data.
- Discover truths about your consumers by asking, watching, and listening.
- Rather than ask a consumer "Why did you make that purchase decision?," say, "I'm interested in hearing more about what you liked with the item," or, "I'd be grateful if you told me more about what you disliked."
- Look for trends, then drill down for details selectively. With numerical performance indicators, look at the mode, median, and range, not only the arithmetic mean.

- If fear is immobilizing you or pressuring you to take premature action, switch briefly to a relatively undemanding retailing task.
- Show caution in using advice from outside consultants which fails to fit your knowledge as a merchant.
- Give outstanding customer service only to the degree that you separate yourself from the competition.
- Steer clear of perfectionism and anger.
- Honor salesmanship by practicing integrity, perseverance, and a well-founded belief that you are capable of using the strengths of your business to achieve high profitability.

11

Customer-Focused Staffing

～

How about this for a silly waste of research money? Three professors and a doctoral student found that work teams have a 20% advantage in performance outcomes when led by someone whose earlobes are mismatched.

The researchers—from Aston University, University of Lancaster, and University of Birmingham,[114] all in the UK—then spent more time developing an explanation for their finding. The explanation begins with musings on why the finding runs counter to what we might expect: We are genetically programmed to like left-right symmetry in people's physical appearance. Evolutionary biologists say it's because an irregular body on the outside can signal abnormal chromosomes inside. In most cultures and organizations, the symmetrical are more likely to be selected as leaders.

Therefore, those without symmetrical features who want to be accepted as leaders must develop skills in persuasion, and this means recognizing others' needs and appealing to others' emotions. That's why the teams led by those with mismatched ear lengths, wrist widths, and finger lengths were more productive.

The lesson for retailers? Even if you and your staff are paragons of balanced left-right beauty, you'll lob more balls over the net profit benchmarks when you show empathy as you coach your store employees.

Just as important, when your staff show respect, concern, and empathy for the consumers, those staff will make more sales.

Customer-focused retail staff bow down before the consumer.

It is 10:00 AM. The doors open at the Tobu Department Store in Tokyo, and as the shoppers enter, the neatly dressed salespersons are standing ramrod straight at their assigned counters. Then as the first shoppers of the day pass, each salesperson bows gracefully.

But as I watched, I didn't see shoppers bowing back.

It's not as if the Japanese are shy about bowing. They bow toward trains arriving at stations. The children bow toward cars that have stopped so the children can cross the street. No, the dearth of reciprocal bowing wasn't because of a lack of habit. Instead, it may have been due, in part, to the substantial time pressure under which many residents of Tokyo operate. The consumers looked more interested in spending their precious moments buying things.

It also was an acknowledgement of power difference. The Tobu employees were bowing down before the power of the shopper to determine if the store would make a profit. The Tobu bowing ritual is a daily reminder. You've an opportunity to deliver that reminder in a different way each payday.

Do you or one of your managers personally deliver the paychecks or direct deposit statements to your staff? Personal delivery provides the opportunity to recognize each employee as an individual contributor to the profitability of your business. Fully use this opportunity.

Make mental and written notes of what your managers are doing well and how they can do even better. Your managers and supervisors should note the same regarding the employees they oversee. Then as the employee is handed the envelope with the paycheck inside, hook it to the performance with a comment or two individualized to that employee.

I'm not suggesting this as a replacement for the daily coaching and the annual performance reviews you'll be conducting. But getting paid is a time for celebration and rededication to boosting business profitability.

It's also a time to recognize where the profit comes from—customers who shop with you. No customers? There's no reason to pull open the curtains at 10 AM.

May I propose how to gift wrap each paycheck or direct deposit notice? In an envelope reading, "Here's a thank you from our customers." To keep top-of-mind awareness for the message, vary the color of the envelopes.

In some situations, the bowing down might take the form of kneeling down. When the waitress at my local Outback restaurant kneeled down next to the table and said, "Hello, my name is Gretchen. I'll be serving you tonight," I did not reply, "I'm honored to meet you. My name is Bruce, and allow me to introduce you to my wife Irene."

Equally odd would have been the server saying, "Hello, my name is Mrs. Fredrickson. I'll be serving you tonight."

Why would that have been odd in a Northern California restaurant? Because I, like other restaurant patrons, envision the waitress or waiter as fulfilling a role which is subservient to mine. The notion behind leaving a tip is that the diner is judging the wait staff. When those role expectations of a superior judging a subordinate are violated, the consumer often becomes uncomfortable. As I noted in Chapter 7's Wells Fargo and Aetna examples, if it's expected that you'll maintain a professional distance, this should be reflected in the marketing and face-to-face phrasing you use.

Researchers at University of North Carolina and Western Carolina University[115] explored what happens to customer tipping when the server draws a smiley face on the check before giving it to the diner. Other research had found that writing a brief thank you leads to higher average tips.

However, in this study, those patrons receiving a bill with a smiley face left a smaller tip percentage than did the patrons getting their bill sans decoration. The smiley face implied a level of familiarity which violated role expectations in the type of retail establishment used for the experiment.

The dampening effect of the happy face—or a brief thank you note—was more when the customer judged the wait staff as not meeting expectations. Satisfied diners getting their checks with the happy face or a note ended up leaving lower tips than did satisfied diners who weren't exposed to the unsolicited doodles. With the dissatisfied diners, the difference between doodles and no doodles was greater still. The inadequate service combined with the effort to seem like an equal with the diner aggravated the dissonance for the customer.

Coach your staff to maintain a respectful social distance from the customer when that's what the customer expects. If you know the customer well in settings outside the retail setting, familiarity like happy faces might be good. If you know the customer well from business inside your store, calling the customer by first name might be welcomed. Otherwise, err on the side of the more formal, and then if the customer gives you permission, loosen up.

As always, there are the exceptions. The "first name rule" may not hold when expectations are for the consumer to be subservient to you. The other rule does, though: If you're a brain surgeon, please refrain from drawing smiley faces or writing "Thanks" next to the incision.

Knowing if your shopper is promotion-focused or prevention-focused helps you choose the right benefits statements to offer when making a sale. The distinction between promotion-focused and prevention-focused also influences how to best supervise the staff who serve those shoppers.

Promotion-focused people play to win, while prevention-focused people play not to lose. At the extreme, the promotion-focused think creatively, welcome risks, and plow through issues quickly. At the other end of the dimension, the prevention-focused anticipate problems and so work meticulously to dig into issues rather than plow through them.

Building on what I discussed in Chapter 1, whether a person is promotion- or prevention-focused can depend on situational factors, such as how long it's been since they've received a paycheck. In Chapter 3, I touched on a related phenomenon when describing how consumers are more likely to form an emotional attachment to an item at retail if the consumer sees the item as fitting their image of their current self—prevention-focused—rather than of the person they aspire to be—promotion-focused.

Most of the people you supervise will display a mix of prevention- and promotion-focused characteristics. However, each of your staff almost surely has a predominant orientation, and each of your staff is highly unlikely to have both a promotion and prevention mindset at the same time.

Identify who's where so you can customize your management style to get maximum effectiveness with minimum effort.

Stories are powerful tools for teaching employees the culture of your business. Promotion-focused staff are most affected when the story is of a role model such as a highly successful salesperson whose methods can be imitated. Prevention-focused staff learn best when hearing about people who, in good faith and with the right intentions, erred, and then what this role model did to turn things right.

Praise the excellent work of the promotion-focused, saying specifics of what they'd done well. Too much talk of shortfalls will discourage them. With the prevention-focused, coach with specifics about how they can avoid or overcome impediments to achieving the objectives both you and they have set. Too much praise for their successes will set off suspicions that you're not leveling with them. They're always on guard.

A reward system in which bonuses are earned beyond a low base amount would be attractive to the promotion-focused. A better fit for the prevention-focused would be a system in which a high base amount is set and deductions are made when there's a shortfall in the staff member's performance. One way to evaluate where each of your employees falls is to ask each which type of system would be preferable to them.

I predict you will find that most of your sales floor people, and probably you yourself, are solidly promotion-focused. That's part of the merchant mindset. You are much more likely to be promotion-focused than is the shopper you're talking to, and that can lead to misdirected sales pitches.

When it comes to your store employees, asking them about themselves helps avoid misunderstandings of all sorts. New employees may hesitate giving you the full story, fearing they'll say something that will jeopardize their continued employment. With this in mind, introduce your inquiries gently.

I'll cite eyesight as an example: A manager at a pharmacy was pleased at his decision to hire Marie as a salesclerk. Older customers seemed much more comfortable asking Marie questions about the merchandise than asking the teenage salesclerks in the store. But the manager noted that Marie seemed to be having some difficulties from being an older person herself: When a shopper would ask Marie for help in reading a package label, Marie often squinted and appeared to lack confidence.

The manager wasn't sure how to approach this. After all, there are laws protecting against age discrimination, he thought. Maybe all Marie needed was an update in her eyeglass prescription. He decided to come at it indirectly. "Marie," he asked, "sometimes I'll assign an employee to pick up pharmaceuticals. Do you need to wear glasses to drive your car?"

"Boss," replied Marie, "I need to wear glasses to *find* my car."

This answer opened up the opportunity for the manager to describe his observation that Marie appeared to be having difficulty reading labels, and the manager's concern that an inaccurate reading of contents or dosage instructions could be a danger to a customer.

I hold a certification called Senior Professional in Human Resources, granted by the Society for Human Resource Management, so I'm keenly aware of the cautions retail managers must exercise in soliciting information from employees in ways which adhere to laws and regulations. Besides, there's so much we want the new employee to know that we frequently find it hard to carve out the time to truly listen.

Respect the rules of employment law and ethical protection of personal privacy. Still, the more we discover about our staff, the more competent we can be in supervising them. Provide employees opportunities to talk, and ask questions which allow staff to share important facts about themselves. Chances are you'll receive the occasional insightful surprise from what you learn.

One story I heard was about Albert, the new hand on deck, who had retired from the U.S. Navy before seeking employment at a retail store. Because of Albert's military background, his direct supervisor was surprised how Albert was habitually late coming to start his shift. Albert was a valued manager once he showed up. He was conscientious. He had a great deal of technical knowledge that he was pleased to share with customers and with other staff. He was skilled in resolving performance problems. Still, the tardiness was becoming more than a nuisance. Other employees, including the group Albert supervised, were complaining.

The manager realized he needed to talk with Albert, and he wanted to do it in a supportive discussion. "Albert," the manager began, "I don't know that much about your past. But I do know you were in the military, where adherence to rules, routines, and teamwork is of top importance. What would your coworkers have said to you if you arrived late for duty?"

Albert smiled slyly. "Most times, they'd say, 'Good day, Admiral.'"

Again, a back-and-forth dialogue yielded an insight fruitful for developing ways to instill your store's values. When all your staff project the values of your business, such as promptness and teamwork, the consistent message instills in shoppers a strong memory of your store. When those values fit what the shopper seeks—the values considerations I discussed in Chapter 3—the potential for selling surges.

The reality is many candidates for employment with you may not share all your values. In fact, the prospective hire—as well as certain employees who have been with you for a while,–might not know what your values are.

As employees identify with a business, their values are open to profound change. There are three levers for this change:

- The employee's economic well-being depends in part on you. Therefore, you have the attention of the employee when you take opportunities to discuss your values.

- For employees who work in your store more than a few hours each week, their job becomes an avenue for socializing with you, other employees, and shoppers. Social learning researchers like Albert Bandura at Stanford University pointed out the strength of personal interactions and behavioral modeling in forming what we call values.

- The third lever is the personal. When you and your staff encourage an employee to discuss how they handled difficulties which have arisen on the job, the employee comes to articulate to themselves a network of values. The result is a consistency across situations.

Increasingly, job seekers use Facebook, Google+, and the rest to size up a retailer as a prospective employer. Sure, they may also be checking out reviews of your store on sites like Yelp, and before applying for employment with you, the diligent applicants will visit your store. But social media channels allow the job seeker to assess the personality of your business from what you, the owner or operator, choose to show and tell.

Include material on your social media sites to reflect the history and the culture of your store. Encourage your current employees to contribute material to the pages, and then comment as the owner/operator on what's been contributed. Invite job seekers to ask questions via the site, and then carve out the time to answer the questions in ways appealing to the types of people you'd like to have working for you.

In hiring interviews, screen prospective employees by presenting a few situations, asking the candidate how they might handle each. These should be real situations that require the person to prioritize among alternatives which reflect values. Be clear with the candidate and in your own mind that there is probably no single best alternative action in each situation. Remember that the person does not yet know your values and that you'll have opportunities to significantly shape those values. But this exercise gives you an impression of how much shaping you'd be taking on.

Once you hire a new employee, mythologize your store. A myth is a special kind of story. Researchers at Boston College and University of Technology-Sydney[116] say that the themes of a myth appeal to psychological needs across cultures. The best retail store myths help explain the origin of the business and give the store a memorable personality based on values.

I've been told that as part of the employee orientation, every new hire at every Nike store hears the magical tale about the track coach in Oregon who poured rubber into his family's waffle iron to produce better shoes for his team's runners—the innovation that inspired the Nike waffle sole. Innovation and the mobilization of available resources are values espoused by Nike stores.

Every employee at every store is told the story? Well, even if the magical tale itself is told truthfully, the report that every employee hears it might qualify as no more than mythical. Never mind. If I've convinced you that it could happen, I've influenced your values, reader. When people accept a myth as possibly true, they are open to being informed and motivated.

Employee appearance projects values to shoppers. Consider an intriguing study from the world of elections. This isn't exactly what political scientists mean by "retail politics," but it's close enough for our purposes:

Successful Republican and Democrat candidates look different. As we saw in Chapter 3, American voters think of successful Republicans in Congress as being reliable and practical. The same voters think of successful Democratic members of Congress as intelligent and empathic. So say researchers at Emory University and University of British Columbia.[117]

Even if they are correct, what does it have to do with running a retail business? As I think you'll see, the link has to do with keeping your credibility.

The researchers began their project by assembling a collection of photos of actual candidates in U.S. congressional races during years 2000, 2002, and 2004. Then they asked the participants in the study to rate a selection of the photos on a number of personality traits. These included traits related to competence, such as reliability, effectiveness, and practicality. The list also included traits associated with intelligence, such as cleverness and talent in discerning the motivations of others. The study participants were not told the name, party affiliation, or congressional district of the candidates in the photos.

The research found that when the physical appearance of a Republican candidate had higher associations with competence than with intelligence, the candidate was more likely to have won her or his election battle. For Democratic candidates, the winning combo was a physical appearance with higher associations to intelligence than to competence.

Why?

Because voters are more likely to believe campaign promises from a candidate fitting the personality image associated with the political party.

If an attack ad during the campaign had been targeted at a Republican candidate who looked more intelligent than competent, votes migrated toward the Democrat. But not so much if the Republican candidate looked more competent than intelligent, as the terms "competence" and "intelligence" had been defined by the researchers. With attack ads lobbed against the Democratic candidates, it worked the other way around.

The effect was strong enough to give an edge to candidates with mugs which fit.

Selling well means persuading other people that what is of benefit to you is also of benefit to them. It's easier when the seller and shopper share a common view of the product, service, idea, or political candidate. Your credibility as an expert helps. So does the credibility of your claim. Claims which are more consistent with the shopper's current view are more likely to persuade.

When you choose to attack stable shopping habits, work within the perceptions of your audiences.

This brings us to dress codes. The clothing you and your staff wear when serving shoppers affects not only the shoppers' impressions of you, but also your impressions of yourselves. Both those can influence your retailing performance.

Researchers at Northwestern University[118] had people put on a white lab coat and complete tests of perceptual attention. Those people told it was a doctor's coat did better on the task than those told it was a painter's coat. Another set of people, who only looked at what they were told was a doctor's coat, but didn't put it on before the task, did not do better than people who never saw the coat. The wearing of the coat combined with the symbolic significance of the coat changed people's thinking and behavior.

A while back, the British Broadcasting Corporation got static for allowing female newsreaders to show lots of leg and the men to wear turned-up jeans. Older viewers recall that when Lord Reith was in charge, even the newsreaders on radio had to wear dinner suits. The objective was to give the news reading the proper gravitas. All this is yet another angle on the theme of contagious magic I discussed in Chapter 2.

There's also an indirect effect. Our wardrobe influences how people respond to us, and that, in turn, influences our retailing behavior. Desmond Morris, whose career work is central to the field of evolutionary psychology, wrote, "It is impossible to wear clothes without transmitting social signals. Every costume tells a story, often a very subtle one, about its wearer. Even those people who insist that they despise attention to clothing, and dress as casually as possible, are making quite specific comments on their social roles and their attitudes towards the culture in which they live."

And their attitudes towards the culture in which they work.

Employee dress standards are part of the service we offer customers. Take a leadership role in deliberatively designing dress codes for your stores, offices, warehouses, and outside sales teams. Think through the functions that employee wardrobe serves for you and incorporate those into the standards.

Eyes will be on your staff, and staff eyes should be on the shoppers. Except for thieves, consumers prefer to be acknowledged when they enter a store or a department within a store. Beyond that initial contact, shoppers want staff available to answer questions. Don't think that the fact the customer tolerates barebones self-service means the customer treasures, or is even satisfied with, barebones self-service. This includes the customer's time at the cash/wrap. Shoppers want it to be quick, but also personable.

Coach your staff to be order getters, not only order takers. They should do this in a way that recognizes a prevailing truth: Customers would much rather buy than be sold. Staff should have the skills of gently, but decisively, spiraling the customer in toward purchases which will both meet the customer's desires and build your retailing profits.

The order getters are skilled at helping customers recognize those desires. Order getters know not to squeeze the customer too hard, since that blocks the free, natural flow of the spiral. At the same time, order getters know not to be so uncertain that the spiral loses its disciplined shape.

Business researchers define the "interception rate" as the percentage of consumers entering a shop who are spoken to by a salesperson working for that shop. "Interception" makes it sound like the salesperson is blocking the person's path, which is a pretty bad way to earn good will. However, the idea of attending to fruitful contact with each shopper is an important one. Such contact enhances the probability of closing a sale and convincing the customer to return to the store.

Researchers at Justus Liebig University and Zeppelin University,[119] in Germany, set out to find what leads shoppers to initiate consultation with a salesperson. They began by verifying that salesperson contact is, in fact, positively related to the amount of money the shopper ends up spending on that store visit.

The researchers then identified major motivators for consultation. Some of the motivators are precisely what you'd suppose. For instance, the shopper knows what they want, but isn't sure which of the offered alternatives to select. Check that you and your staff are easily available on the sales floor and that the available staff either have the knowledge to answer shopper questions or know where to fetch the answers. But even here, the research findings provide a refinement: To raise the interception rate, be able to sense how much time and mental energy the person wants to spend considering the shopping decision. If a shopper fears that you'll be giving too much information, they'll avoid asking you.

Other of the motivators make sense when you think about them, but you might not have been thinking about them. For instance, the shopper is finding the store visit enjoyable, and so is open to conversation with the store staff. Create within the minds of your shoppers an image of what consumer researchers call "a third place." This is an environment in addition to home and work which is appealing because it feels comfortable. Give an authentic sense of family to your customers. Some retail consultants say, "Make our customers feel like family." I prefer, "Give a sense of family," because research findings seem clear that for maximum profitability, you want to be sure to keep the interactions a business relationship. Don't promise more than you'll deliver. That wouldn't be authentic.

Be sure your customers recognize the benefits that came from their purchases. With so much going on in their busy lives, the purchaser can too easily forget to give credit to a service or product for the benefits they obtained. And sales staff can too easily forget to hook inside the customer's mind the effect to the cause.

This can be because sales staff are, like the customers, very busy. Yet there's another reason as well: Sales staff who are thoroughly familiar with how nicely a particular item produces benefits can take it for granted that the customer knows, too.

Customers usually want specifications pre-purchase, but after making the purchase, they're usually seeking post-purchase reassurance. So right after the purchase, tell the customer that they've made a good decision.

Then when the customer returns to your store later or contacts you to place a telephone or ecommerce order, assume they are now ready to sample and to shop. Deliver a different sort of reassurance about their prior purchase: Emphasize cause and effect. Point out to them how what they obtained from you produced benefits important to them.

Do you recall what they bought? If so, ask a question like, "How did you feel the evening after you had your last massage here?" or "How did that carpeting work out for you in your family room?"

If you don't recall the prior purchase and can't promptly obtain the information from your customer database, start with, "What are some of your most recent purchases from us?" It's better to assume the person is a prior customer and be wrong than to assume the person has never shopped with you before and insult a loyal client.

Being able to think on your feet is an important characteristic for your employees in a broader sense, too. Customer Need Knowledge (CNK) is the extent to which a frontline employee in a store—the one who serves customers face-to-face—accurately and promptly identifies each customer's needs and desires. As you'd expect, the research clearly finds that when the CNK of employees in a store is higher, customers tend to be more satisfied and to say they've gotten better value from their purchases. An employee with high CNK pays close attention to each customer they're with and considers each shopper transaction as an intriguing mystery to be solved.

One way to increase the CNK of your store's staff is to manage employee turnover. Retailing has higher employee turnover than most other types of business. Some turnover in any organization is good. By bringing in new ideas, turnover heads off inbreeding and stagnation. Turnover can disrupt CNK, though. A top facilitator of CNK is the customer having dealt with the employee over a period of time. Longer-term employees get more opportunity to learn what a store's target markets are like and will like. When consumers talk about why they prefer shopping at small to midsize retailers rather than at large stores or online, they'll often say they enjoy seeing familiar faces.

At the same time, recognize and correct for the ways in which your target markets are different from your sales staff. CNK is less when there's a large age discrepancy between the salesperson and that salesperson's typical customers. This argues for hiring employees who are similar in age to your typical customers. You'll want to be sure those employees also can learn retailing skills and that you obey antidiscrimination employment law. Working at it from the other direction, use the characteristics of your talented employees to help you attract customers like them.

It's an error to believe that research has uniformly found substantial benefits when the racial/ethnic characteristics of the employees and target customers closely match. In truth, the research literature has yielded inconsistent answers to the question. The reason for inconsistent results is that the match doesn't affect profitability directly, but does it indirectly by increasing customer satisfaction. If other factors disrupt customer satisfaction, the racial/ethnic match won't help sales revenues.

Some might think that the match is helpful only when there are many minority customers. Yes, it is most strong then, because minority shoppers are especially likely to have received inferior customer service in the past from salespeople who do not share the shopper's racial/ethnic characteristics. When minority shoppers see minority employees, the shoppers consider this a sign they'll receive good service.[120] However, the match-advantage effect also holds true when there are few minority customers. The general point is that shoppers are more satisfied when dealing with salespeople they see as being like themselves because they believe they'll be respected for who they are.

There's even been research about serving ugly shoppers. It might be difficult for you and your staff to look directly at someone is who physically quite unattractive. But when serving an ugly shopper, check yourself as to whether you're doing a proper job of carefully looking after the sales potential.

A good body of consumer behavior research confirms that good bodies draw special attention in the store. The physically attractive get served more quickly than those of average appearance, and they are more likely to have special requests honored. Whereas onlookers may stigmatize customers who are using small-denomination discount coupons, those who are highly attractive don't get stigmatized, according to research at University of Alberta and University of Manitoba.[121]

Being physically unattractive brings worse than neutral or lackadaisical attention. Research findings from Michigan State University and University of Notre Dame[122] indicate that these shoppers will be the targets of rudeness and exploitation. The cause-and-effect are not clear. It's possible, for example, that a long history of being shunned or ridiculed has generated from physical ugliness an interpersonal ugliness which brings out the worst in salespeople. Also please keep in mind that the study conclusions refer to tendencies, not what's true in every case.

Still, the contribution of the research is in reminding us of the strength and the subconscious quality of the tendency. The best response? I'll name it "The Phantom of the Opera Method." In the Andrew Lloyd Weber production, when Christine Daaé looks through and beyond her repulsion at the appearance of Phantom, she expresses tenderness.

I wouldn't advise that you or your sales staff hug any shopper you don't know well, regardless of the shopper's degree of physical appeal or your feelings of tenderness. However, a virtual hug could work fine. Shake hands, bump fists, place a hand on the arm, gently extend your hands toward the shopper with palms facing up as if you'd like to lift up their spirits—whatever is culturally and socially appropriate to project a welcome. Then maintain the style of culturally appropriate eye contact to stay psychologically in touch.

Moving through and beyond the subconscious impulse to look away empowers us to honor the value of each individual who enters our stores. That's surely helpful for a good living.

Also helpful for a good living is handling your employee's shortfalls with respect, concern, and empathy. Focus on fixing the problem rather than on fixing the blame. Let's say something has gone wrong in your retail business. It's serious enough that you've switched from open minds mode—in which you invite creative ideas—or open roads mode—in which you're moving ahead assertively—to open wounds mode—in which you must take prompt, decisive corrective action.

Now after the panic eases, who do you blame for what went wrong?

Maybe nobody. Holding people responsible is different from fixing blame. Estimates by psychologists at New York University and University of Tulsa[123] suggest that about 70% of retail employees will do less well in a store like yours if you put more emphasis on fixing the blame for the problem than on fixing the problem which caused the setback.

The researchers observed the thinking and behavior set off by harshly blaming retail employees for serious problems that developed in the business. Some employees denied that failure occurred or denied any responsibility for it. Such employees then began distorting everyday business occurrences so as to avoid confronting problems. Other employees accepted some responsibility, but deflected most of the responsibility to other people or to unforeseeable circumstances. These employees were then too quick to sense only the criticism when given constructive advice. Still others announced their responsibility in order to brag about the corrective actions they'd taken. These employee might aim to impress managers excessively, sabotaging teamwork. And still others wallowed in self-blame out of proportion to their actual responsibility. This group overreacted to even minor mistakes afterwards, withdrawing from necessary risk-taking, and prematurely labeling setbacks as failures.

Guilt and shame are powerful emotions which can lead to the dysfunctional consequences identified by the researchers. Embarrassment is a milder emotion in which the employee still accepts both responsibility and that others know about the incident.

As problems arise in your retail business, hammer out the difficulties in supportive ways. Use your hammer to repair the shortfalls, not to pound your valuable staff—and consequently, their staff morale—into the ground. Stop at embarrassment, short of guilt or shame.

A number of years ago, I obtained a consulting contract to write content for Employee Appraiser software. I provided suggestions which were generated for employees and their supervisors when performance problems of various sorts arouse.

In completing the assignment, I developed an outline I called the Nine-Layer Onion. Subsequently, my RIMtailing clients and my students in "Performance Management" classes I taught at University of Nevada-Reno College of Extended Studies told me they found the questions and answers generated by the Nine-Layer Onion to be useful.

When faced with an employee performance problem which impedes your store profitability, peel away the layers one-by-one until you find the cause and have taken effective corrective action. At each layer, shape the employee's behavior with well-formed questions to yourself:

- **Situational problem.** Does this appear to be a short-term problem? If so, put your energies into addressing other issues while keeping an eye on the employee.
- **Expectations.** How well have you communicated to the employee specifically what you expect? Busy retailers too often assume that new employees are aware of the difficulties caused by flawed behavior.

- **Trust.** Does the employee trust what you're saying? A store's mission, vision, and values statements come across as meaningless if the owner/operator fails to exemplify them.

- **Resources.** Does the employee have sufficient time to learn the skills or sufficient authority to carry out the behaviors you're wanting?

- **Incentive/disincentive ratio.** Are the incentives for doing what you ask sufficient to overcome the disincentives? A disincentive might be social rejection by coworkers for raising the bar. Or it might be time away from family.

- **Self-management skills.** For instance, is the employee a perfectionist who spends too much time on a task? If self-management is the issue, teach project management skills.

- **Technical skills.** Yes, this should be obvious at first, but it often lies buried.

- **Interpersonal skills.** Do you find yourself calling it a problem of "attitude"? Because attitude is difficult to discuss with an employee, it often works best to leave it alone and address the earlier layers first. If you do get to this point, describe to the employee a set of behaviors within specific situations as examples of what you want rather than talking in terms of attitudes.

- **Disability.** If all else hasn't corrected the problem, does the employee have a disability as defined in the American with Disabilities Act? Before probing here, be sure you know your legal obligations to accommodate disabilities.

In my experience, unclear expectations—the second layer of the onion—are a common problem when it comes to employee honesty. Your employees should know what you define as dishonesty and what to expect if they are found to have acted in a dishonest manner. This has become more important because of compelling evidence that a substantial percentage of young people who are entering the retailing workforce are accustomed to cheating. University of Central Florida—America's third-largest campus as measured by student enrollment at the time of the survey—reported that about 60% of college undergraduates admitted to cheating on assignments or exams. And I'm figuring that 60% didn't include those who lied when they said they hadn't cheated!

Decide on the degree of honesty you want your store to project. Does this sound to you like a strange suggestion, retailer? Well, the fact is that some customers prefer to deal with salespeople who are what I call Rascals. The Rascal exploits other people. Especially in individualistic cultures like the U.S. and Great Britain, consumers are fascinated with famous rascals. When the retail personality you aim for includes "exciting" and your target markets include people from individualistic cultures, you might decide to have your salespeople project an image of testing the limits and squeezing around authority. Petty cheating is tolerated.

Once you've decided on the degree of honesty you want your store to project, be as sure as you can that employees know your expectations. This in itself is a bit tricky, since retail owners/operators who tolerate or even encourage Rascal behavior may be unlikely to say that out loud. You can communicate your expectations through your own behavior. Do you fudge the truth when talking to employees and then laugh it off? Are you obvious about using store equipment and supplies for non-business purposes?

Then there's another layer of possible confusion: You might have different expectations of strict honesty for different types of employees. Maybe your store culture is such that it's fine for salespeople to tell customers, "I'm 100% sure this product is ideally suited for you," even if they aren't 100% sure. But you probably don't want your bookkeeper to say, "I'm sure the store cashiers were 100% accurate last month," when your bookkeeper really isn't that certain at all.

Because of these sources of confusion, also communicate your expectations via consequences. Have consistent consequences for any dishonesty that is not acceptable. Minimize the surprises. Provide your staff opportunities to discover what is okay and what's not.

It's bad when employees steal from you. How about when they steal from your customers?

Researchers at Texas Christian University[124] set up their experimental situation by leaving loose change inside a car brought to a full service car wash. In some of the cars, the researchers had also placed, on the front seat, a copy of *Maxim* magazine with its photos of scantily dressed women, and on the floor, a crushed beer can. The research question was whether these cars had more money stolen than from debris-free cars.

The findings: In the cleaner cars, cash was taken about 35% of the time. In the cars with the magazine and crushed can, the thievery rate was double that.

The researchers' explanation is that employees at the car wash probably considered the drivers of cars with *Maxim* and beer as morally deviant and therefore more suitable to be victimized.

One response I have to this is that all customers, even those who drink and gawk, deserve to be treated with integrity. Calling shoppers deviant becomes a license for prejudice.

Another response is that those more likely to have money stolen may have been seen as messy, not morally deviant. Hey, you take your vehicle to the car wash for the full-deal service and it looks like you didn't notice you left a beer can and magazine in the front seat. Odds are fair you won't notice it if, while removing the can and closing the magazine, I also tidy up some of your loose change.

"The money was asking to be taken," some retail employees might say. After all, even in the non-*Maxim* no-beer-can car, money was stolen a third of the time.

Now let's bring the discussion back to include the theft of merchandise or cash from you. Keep the storage areas in your store unlocked only to the degree necessary. Require an employee who is thinking of stealing to acknowledge that the thievery will involve a series of dishonest steps. In training, periodically give evidence of how employee theft damages the organization. Do not discuss the topic at every training session, though. The high frequency makes thievery seem to your employees almost routinely expected. Inform employees you'll be conducting surprise audits. At the car wash, employees could be told there will be "loose change temptation" checks from time to time.

There are flavors of dishonesty which are more subtle. For instance, how big a bite is torn out from your profitability by "sweethearting"? That word with so many pleasant associations has a sinister meaning in the realm of retailing. Sweethearting refers to a store employee giving away products for free or at a deep price cut with plans to get, in return, an extra tip, increased social status, or a product for free or at a deep price cut from the sweethearting recipient.

Policies which allow employees to give discounts to their family members can build staff loyalty. Allowing employees to reward good customers with free gifts can increase shopping cart totals and cultivate repeat business. But these are done with the knowledge of the owner/operator, who should be tracking whether the discounts and freebies achieve the intended objectives.

Stab sweethearting. Set policies which are unambiguous and easily understood. What sorts of items can be given away or deeply discounted? Which employees are granted the discretion to do this and under what circumstances? What practices, such as exchanging one discount for another, are forbidden? To audit the extent and the effectiveness of the practices, what degree of reporting and accountability are required from those employees? Be careful that the reporting process isn't overly burdensome, since this will discourage employee initiative and the use of appropriate gifting.

Enforce the policies by punishing offenders in proportion to the offense. What strikes staff as excessive severity of punishment is not associated with a decrease in subsequent sweethearting, and it generates resentments toward you among your staff.

When it comes to responding to requests from shoppers and customers, empower your employees. Yet probably not every single one of your employees. There are those who are better able to make the right decisions than are others. Much of it has to do with amount of experience and the training. If your employees do go beyond what the store policies say, they must let their supervisor know so the issue can be discussed. These are opportunities for teaching, learning, and possibly revising.

Many of the requests made by shoppers and customers are "fuzzy." The entreaties are slightly or somewhat outside store policy, but not blatantly wrong. The shopper who looks familiar comes in as soon as the store opens, asking for the sale price which expired yesterday. The customer who doesn't look familiar comes in at a busy time asking you to teach his wife right then how to use the technology he purchased.

Watch employees in action so you personally see that fuzzy requests are being handled in the ways you prefer. When they are, praise the employee with specific feedback. Use staff meetings, huddles at the start of each workday, and other opportunities to clearly say what you expect of your employees. Don't assume that one discussion is enough for forever. The human brain doesn't work that way.

When you address employee performance problems more than engage in blame and when you peel away possible causes layer-by-layer, you set an example for your store staff treating each other respectfully. This reduces the chances for the type of thing which went wrong, with the best of management intentions, in this situation:

A customer bursts into the store, rushes toward a salesperson, and starts complaining loudly about defects in a product she'd purchased. The salesperson calmly replies, "What would you like me to do to make things right for you?"

In response, the customer roars, "Look, I'm upset. You don't sound like you're taking me seriously. I want to talk to a manager." The salesperson says, "I'll get you a manager. Please wait just a minute or two." The salesperson radios for a manager, saying, "I've a customer who is very dissatisfied and would like to talk to a manager."

As soon as the manager arrives, he immediately says to the customer, "What would you like me to do to make things right for you?" For a moment, there is silence. Then both the salesperson and the manager notice the customer's nostrils flaring as she says, "You people keep repeating yourselves. Your salesperson here didn't even ask me what my problem really is."

At that, the manager turns, with a combination of irritation and frustration, away from the customer and toward the salesperson to say, with pointed finger, "Our customers are our most important asset. How could you not ask the customer what the problem is? This customer deserves better than that. This is not the first time you've done something like this."

According to findings by researchers at University of Southern California,[125] about 40% of retail consumers report that at least once each month, they see a store employee treat another store employee so rudely that the consumer becomes very uncomfortable to the point of not wanting to continue patronizing that store.

Here, the manager aimed to show the customer she was being respected. But this message was severely undercut in front of the customer by the failure of the manager to show respect to the salesperson.

Retail staff too often fail to recognize that how each of them interacts with the shopper influences how the shopper interprets the interactions with other staff. Let's say a sales clerk looks up at the approaching shopper and smiles gently. If that event had been preceded by a sincere greeting from the cashier as the shopper entered the store, the shopper is likely to consider the salesperson's smile to be sincere and welcoming. This is less likely if the shopper had received no more than a cold stare from the cashier when entering the store. It's related to the emotion contagion I discussed in Chapter 5.

Researchers at University of Miami and University of Southern California[126] explored how consumers infer the quality of service expected in settings like hotels. What's the effect of flawed service at the front desk on the guest's expectations when they consider using the hotel's tour arrangements? A major factor was managerial control. If the guest sees the same manager talking to the front desk and the concierge, the guest becomes more likely to conclude that what holds true for one holds true for the other. This is a sensible assumption, to be sure. The similarity principle also holds when it comes to employee wardrobe. If your personnel dress in a distinctive store outfit, the impact of spreading impressions is greater.

When two staff members work physically close to each other, the consumer generalizes impressions from one to the other more strongly. This similarly applies to contiguity in time, when the interactions with one staff member come soon after prior interactions with the other staff member.

Regularly emphasize to yourself and your staff how each of you shares the responsibility for initiating and maintaining a sincere welcome. It's a part of what organizational psychologists call "task identity," seeing to it that employees recognize they're all in it together and their work achieves top significance only when duties overlap.

I began this chapter by reporting to you an actual research study which seemed to be a substantial waste of time. I end the chapter using a wildly improbable fictitious tale on a parallel theme.

As the shop owner looked out the front window of her store, she saw a man digging a hole in the median strip of the wide street. Then the man moved about thirty feet beyond the pile of dirt and dug another hole.

When done with that one, he again moved on about thirty feet from the second dirt pile and dug a third hole.

An hour later, she looked out the window again, only to see another man shoveling the pile of dirt back into the hole. Sure enough, after filling in the first hole, he moved on to the second hole, filled in that one, and then on to the third hole.

The shopkeeper couldn't contain her curiosity about what appeared to be some monumental waste of city workers' time. She crossed the street to the median, walked up to the man filling in the third hole, and asked him to explain.

"Oh," he began, with a nod which indicated he'd heard the questions before. "We have a system here. My buddy digs out the dirt from the hole, my other buddy puts a tree in the hole, and then I come along and fill in the hole with the dirt."

"There's no tree there!," the woman exclaimed.

"Yea, that guy's out sick today. But the other two of us still have our jobs to get done."

RIMinders

- Deliver paychecks and direct deposit notices to employees in envelopes labeled "Here's a thank you from our customers."
- Take the time to learn about your employees, while respecting the rules of employment law and ethical protection of personal privacy. For each employee, determine if the individual is more interested in achieving wins or more interested in avoiding losses.
- Set a dress code for employees based on the profitability functions of your employees' appearance.
- Remind customers of the benefits that came or will come with their purchases.
- Minimize differences between the characteristics of your sales staff and the characteristics of your target customers.
- Unambiguously state your expectations to employees, especially when it comes to the definition of honesty and the consequences for the business and the individual employee of dishonesty.

- Place a higher priority on fixing each problem than on fixing the blame.
- Coach your store employees to show respect, concern, and empathy for their fellow employees and for the shoppers they serve together.
- Show respect, concern, and empathy as you coach your store employees to reflect the values of your store and to be order getters, not only order takers.

12

Act & Acknowledge

~

I've written this book as a call to action for you, retailer. You might note that the entry in the index with the most page numbers after it is "RIMinders," pointing you to the specific action steps at the end of Chapters 1 through 11. All those steps are based on solid consumer research. Some of the studies I've cited are classics which continue to provide profitable guidance, while others are new enough to take account of how opportunities for educated retailers are ever-changing. The research resources range in publication year from 1972 through 2014.

Still, as you're reading this right now, circumstances will have changed further. I encourage you to make use of my RIMtailing blog, at www.rimtailing.blogspot.com, where I publish updates using the latest research findings. The blog has a search utility to allow you to quickly locate tips most relevant to your situation, and I end most of my postings with links to related postings. *Sell Well* establishes an integrated foundation for action that you wouldn't get from the RIMtailing blog on its own, and the blog builds on that foundation by keeping you current.

The entry in the index with the second-most page numbers after it is "Respect." Respectful acknowledgement of the interests of our consumers is the best underpinning for all the profitability tactics I'm giving you. And I give them to you with my respectful gratitude toward the researchers who conducted the studies which stimulated my recommendations, toward the institutions that hosted the studies, and toward the professional publications whose editors peer-reviewed the studies to ensure high quality. Many of those researchers, institutions, and publications aren't named by me in this book. That's because I've chosen to cite only selected projects which typify what's been discovered. I dislike unnecessary repetition.

An even greater abundance of respect and gratitude goes toward the retailers who have participated in my training sessions and/or received my consultation, implemented some of the ideas you've read about here, and then told me how it worked out. Not everything suggested by the research pays off in the store. Moreover, for maximum payoff, the tactics need to be personalized to fit the characteristics of the particular business.

As you put into action the ideas in *Sell Well* for yourself and assess the consequences, please email me at RIMtailing@gmail.com to tell me how to give even better advice to you and your colleagues next time around.

I welcome suggestions in the same spirit that I encourage you to welcome suggestions from the stakeholders in your business's success. Even when you don't take the advice, your responses are an opportunity to think through why you're doing what you're doing. And that is the spirit with which I acknowledge the contributions to this book by those who reviewed the text before publication. Most distinctive for me among my reviewers is retired California State Compensation Insurance Fund executive vice president Bernard I. Freedman, who began his career selling insurance. Now 97 years old, he brought a wealth of business experience, consumer experience, and readership experience to the endeavor of critiquing what I'd written.

My special thanks to Bernie.

Research Resources

1 Cassie Mogilner, Jennifer Aaker & Sepandar Kamvar. "How Happiness Impacts Choice." *Journal of Consumer Research*. August 2012.

2 Xinyue Zhou, Kathleen D. Vohs & Roy F. Baumeister. "The Symbolic Power of Money: Reminders of Money Alter Social Distress and Physical Pain." *Psychological Science*. June 2009.

3 Yeşim Orhun & Oleg Urminsky. "Conditional Projection: How Own Evaluations Influence Beliefs About Others Whose Choices Are Known." *Journal of Marketing Research*. February 2013.

4 Andrew D. Gershoff, Ashesh Mukherjee & Anirban Mukhopadhyay. "What's Not to Like? Preference Asymmetry in the False Consensus Effect." *Journal of Consumer Research*. June 2008.

5 Andrew D. Gershoff & Johnathan J. Koehler. "Safety First? The Role of Emotion in Safety Product Betrayal Aversion." *Journal of Consumer Research*. June 2011.

6 Sanjay Sood & Xavier Dreze. "Brand Extensions of Experiential Goods: Movie Sequel Evaluations." *Journal of Consumer Research*. December 2006.

7 Mario Pandelaere, Barbara Briers & Christophe Lembregts. "How to Make a 29% Increase Look Bigger: The Unit Effect in Option Comparisons." *Journal of Consumer Research*. August 2011.

8 Himanshu Mishra, Arul Mishra & Dhananjay Nayakankuppam. "How Salary Receipt Affects Consumers' Regulatory Motivations and Product Preferences." *Journal of Marketing*. September 2010.

9 Kristina Durante, Vladas Griskeviciu, Sarah E. Hill, Carin Perilloux & Norman P. Li. "Ovulation, Female Competition, and Product Choice: Hormonal Influences on Consumer Behavior." *Journal of Consumer Research*. April 2011.

10 Yuval Rottenstreich, Sanjay Sood & Lyle Brenner. "Feeling and Thinking in Memory-Based Versus Stimulus-Based Choices." *Journal of Consumer Research*. March 2007.

11 Susan Jung Grant, Prashant Malaviya & Brian Sternthal. "The Influence of Negation on Product Evaluations." *Journal of Consumer Research*. December 2004.

12 George E. Newman, Gil Diesendruck & Paul Bloom. "Celebrity Contagion and the Value of Objects." *Journal of Consumer Research*. August 2011.

13 Sally Linkenauger. "You'll Golf Better If You Think Tiger Has Used Your Clubs." *Harvard Business Review.* July/August 2012.

14 Karen V. Fernandez & John L. Lastovicka. "Making Magic: Fetishes in Contemporary Consumption." *Journal of Consumer Research*. August 2011.

15 Rob M.A. Nelissen & Marijn H.C. Meijers. "Social Benefits of Luxury Brands as Costly Signals of Wealth and Status." *Evolution and Human Behavior.* September 2011.

16 Jonah Berger & Morgan Ward. "Subtle Signals of Inconspicuous Consumption." *Journal of Consumer Research*. December 2010.

17 Blakeley B. Mcshane, Eric T. Bradlow & Jonah Berger. "Visual Influence and Social Groups." *Journal of Marketing Research*. December 2012.

18 Ji Kyung Park & Deborah Roedder John. "Got to Get You into My Life: Do Brand Personalities Rub Off on Consumers?" *Journal of Consumer Research*. February 2011.

19 Aaron R. Brough & Alexander Chernev. "When Opposites Detract: Categorical Reasoning and Subtractive Valuations of Product Combinations." *Journal of Consumer Research*. August 2012.

20 Amitav Chakravarti & Chris Janiszewski. "The Influence of Generic Advertising on Brand Preferences." *Journal of Consumer Research*. March 2004.

21 S. Ratneshwar, Lawrence W. Barsalou, Cornelia Pechmann & Melissa Moore. "Goal-Derived Categories: The Role of Personal and Situational Goals in Category Representations." *Journal of Consumer Psychology.* 10(3). 2001.

22 David A. Houston & Steven J. Sherman. "Cancellation and Focus: The Role of Shared and Unique Features in the Choice Process." *Journal of Experimental Social Psychology.* July 1995.

23 Keith Wilcox, Anne L. Roggeveen & Dhruv Grewal. "Shall I Tell You Now or Later? Assimilation and Contrast in the Evaluation of Experiential Products." *Journal of Consumer Research*. December 2011.

24 Rajneesh Suri & Mrugank V. Thakor. "'Made in Country' Versus 'Made in County': Effects of Local Manufacturing Origins on Price Perceptions." *Psychology & Marketing*. February 2013.

25 Carl McDaniel & R.C. Baker. "Convenience Food Packaging and the Perception of Product Quality." *Journal of Marketing*. October 1977.

26 Sarah Kim & Aparna A. Labroo. "From 'Inherent Value' to 'Incentive Value': When and Why Non-Instrumental Effort Enhances Consumer Preference." *Journal of Consumer Research*. December 2011.

27 Kurt A. Carlson & Jacqueline M. Conard. "The Last Name Effect: How Last Name Influences Acquisition Timing." *Journal of Consumer Research*. August 2011.

28 Neeru Paharia, Anat Keinan, Jill Avery & Juliet B. Schor. "The Underdog Effect: The Marketing of Disadvantage and Determination through Brand Biography." *Journal of Consumer Research*. February 2011.

29 Goitom Tesfom & Nancy Birch. "Do They Buy for Their Dogs the Way They Buy for Themselves?" *Psychology & Marketing*. September 2010.

30 Itamar Simonson & Aner Sela. "On the Heritability of Consumer Decision Making: An Exploratory Approach for Studying Genetic

Effects on Judgment and Choice." *Journal of Consumer Research*. April 2011.

31 Romana Khan, Kanishka Misra & Vishal Singh. "Ideology and Brand Consumption." *Psychological Science*. March 2013.

32 Scott I. Rick, Cynthia E. Cryder & George Loewenstein. "Tightwads and Spendthrifts." *Journal of Consumer Research*. April 2008.

33 Shibo Li, Baohong Sun & Alan L. Montgomery. "Cross-Selling the Right Product to the Right Customer at the Right Time." *Journal of Marketing Research*. August 2011.

34 Jinhee Choi & Ayelet Fishbach. "Choice as an End Versus a Means." *Journal of Marketing Research*. June 2011.

35 Morgan K. Ward & Susan M. Broniarczyk. "It's Not Me, It's You: How Gift Giving Creates Giver Identity Threat as a Function of Social Closeness." *Journal of Consumer Research*. June 2011.

36 Keri L. Kettle & Gerald Häubl. "The Signature Effect: Signing Influences Consumption-Related Behavior by Priming Self-Identity." *Journal of Consumer Research*. October 2011.

37 Lucia Malär, Harley Krohmer, Wayne D. Hoyer & Bettina Nyffenegger. "Emotional Brand Attachment and Brand Personality: The Relative Importance of the Actual and the Ideal Self." *Journal of Marketing*. July 2011.

38 Elaine Chan & Jaideep Sengupta. "Insincere Flattery Actually Works: A Dual Attitudes Perspective." *Journal of Marketing Research*. February 2010.

39 Jozef M. Nuttin, Jr. "Affective Consequences of Mere Ownership: The Name Letter Effect in Twelve European Languages." *European Journal of Social Psychology*. October/December 1987.

40 Keith S. Coulter & Dhruv Grewal. "Name-Letters and Birthday-Numbers: Implicit Egotism Effects in Pricing." *Journal of Marketing*. May 2014.

41 Marshall Fisher & Ramnath Vaidyanathan. "Which Products Should You Stock?" *Harvard Business Review*. November 2012.

42 Denish Shah, V. Kumar & Kihyun Hannah Kim. "Managing Customer Profits: The Power of Habits." *Journal of Marketing Research*. December 2014.

43 Claudia Gilleßen, Petra Berkholz & Rainer Stamminger. "Manual Dishwashing Process—A Pre-Assigned Behaviour?" *International Journal of Consumer Studies*. August 2012.

44 Jiska Eelen, Siegfried Dewitte & Luk Warlop. "Situated Embodied Cognition: Monitoring Orientation Cues Affects Product Evaluation and Choice." *Journal of Consumer Psychology*. October 2013.

45 Joydeep Srivastava & Shweta Oza. "Effect of Response Time on Perceptions of Bargaining Outcomes." *Journal of Consumer Research*. September 2006.

46 David Gal. "A Mouthwatering Prospect: Salivation to Material Reward." *Journal of Consumer Research*. April 2012.

47 Gerald J. Gorn. "The Effects of Music in Advertising on Choice Behavior: A Classical Conditioning Approach." *Journal of Marketing*. Winter 1982.

48 Ravi Dhar, Joel Huber & Uzma Khan. "The Shopping Momentum Effect." *Journal of Marketing Research*. August 2007.

49 Sukki Yoon & Patrick Vargas. "'No More' Leads to 'Want More,' But 'No Less' Leads to 'Want Less': Consumers' Counterfactual Thinking When Faced with Quantity Restriction Discounts." *Journal of Consumer Behaviour*. March 2011.

50 Nicolas Gueguen, Celine Jacob & Angelique Martin. "Mimicry in Social Interaction: Its Effect on Human Judgment and Behavior." *European Journal of Social Sciences*. April 2009.

51 Cristel Antonia Russell & Sidney J. Levy. "The Temporal and Focal Dynamics of Volitional Re-Consumption: A Phenomenological Investigation of Repeated Hedonic Experiences." *Journal of Consumer Research*. August 2012.

52 Andreas B. Eisingerich & Leslie Boehm. "Hospital Visitors Ask for More Shopping Outlets." *Harvard Business Review*. September 2009.

53 Daniel J. Howard & Roger A. Kerin. "Changing Your Mind About Seeing a Brand that You Never Saw: Implications For Brand Attitudes." *Psychology & Marketing*. February 2011.

54 Ashwani Monga & Rajesh Bagchi. "Years, Months, and Days Versus 1, 12, and 365: The Influence of Units versus Numbers." *Journal of Consumer Research*. June 2012.

55 Christophe Lembregts & Mario Pandelaere. "Are All Units Created Equal? The Effect of Default Units on Product Evaluations." *Journal of Consumer Research*. April 2013.

56 John D. Bransford, J. Richard Barclay & Jeffery J. Franks. "Sentence Memory: A Constructive Versus Interpretive Approach." *Cognitive Psychology*. April 1972.

57 Angela Y. Lee & Aparna A. Labroo. "The Effect of Conceptual and Perceptual Fluency on Affective Judgment." *Journal of Marketing Research*. May 2004.

58 Dan King & Chris Janiszewski. "The Sources and Consequences of the Fluent Processing of Numbers." *Journal of Marketing Research*. April 2011.

59 Bram Van den Bergh, Julien Schmitt & Luk Warlop. "Embodied Myopia." *Journal of Marketing Research*. December 2011.

60 Alastair G. Tombs & Janet R. McColl-Kennedy. "Third Party Customers Infecting Other Customers for Better or for Worse." *Psychology & Marketing*. March 2013.

61 Piotr Winkielman, Kent C. Berridge & Julia L. Wilbarger. "Unconscious Affective Reactions to Masked Happy Versus Angry Faces Influence Consumption Behavior and Judgments of Value." *Personality and Social Psychology Bulletin*. January 2005.

62 Sam K. Hui, J. Jeffrey Inman, Yanliu Huang & Jacob Suher. "The Effect of In-Store Travel Distance on Unplanned Spending: Applications to Mobile Promotion Strategies." *Journal of Marketing*. March 2013.

63 Richard C. Anderson, Ralph E. Reynolds, Diane L. Schallert & Ernest T. Goetz. "Frameworks for Comprehending Discourse." *American Educational Research Journal*. September 1977.

64 Philip Stanley Grant, Bal Anjali & Michael Parent. "Operatic Flash Mob: Consumer Arousal, Connectedness, and Emotion." *Journal of Consumer Behaviour*. May/June 2012.

65 Daniel Read & George Loewenstein. "Diversification Bias: Explaining the Discrepancy in Variety Seeking Between Combined and Separated Choices." *Journal of Experimental Psychology: Applied*. March 1995.

66 Richard G. Netemeyer, Carrie M. Heilman & James G. Maxham III. "The Impact of a New Retail Brand In-Store Boutique and Its Perceived

Fit with the Parent Retail Brand on Store Performance and Customer Spending." *Journal of Retailing*. December 2012.

67 Hillary J.D. Wiener & Tanya L. Chartrand. "The Effect of Voice Quality on Ad Efficacy." *Psychology & Marketing*. July 2014.

68 Roy E Baumeister, Ellen Bratslavsky, Mark Muraven & Dianne M. Tice. "Ego Depletion: Is the Active Self a Limited Resource?" *Journal of Personality and Social Psychology*. May 1998.

69 Leif D. Nelson, Tom Meyvis & Jeff Galak. "Enhancing the Television-Viewing Experience Through Commercial Interruptions." *Journal of Consumer Research*. August 2009.

70 Hung-Chang Chiu, Yi-Ching Hsieh & Yi-Chu Kuo. "How to Align Your Brand Stories with Your Products." *Journal of Retailing*. June 2012.

71 Daniel Wentzel, Torsten Tomczak & Andreas Herrmann. "The Moderating Effect of Manipulative Intent and Cognitive Resources on the Evaluation of Narrative Ads." *Psychology & Marketing*. May 2010.

72 Andrew E. Wilson & Peter R. Darke. "The Optimistic Trust Effect: Use of Belief in a Just World to Cope with Decision." *Journal of Consumer Research*. October 2012.

73 Bob M. Fennis, Loes Janssen & Kathleen D. Vohs. "Acts of Benevolence: A Limited-Resource Account of Compliance with Charitable Requests." *Journal of Consumer Research*. April 2009.

74 Y. Charles Zhang & Norbert Schwarz. "How and Why One Year Differs from 365 Days: A Conversational Logic Analysis of Inferences from the Granularity of Quantitative Expressions." *Journal of Consumer Research*. August 2012.

75 Eryn J. Newman, Maryanne Garry, Daniel M. Bernstein, Justin Kantner & D. Stephen Lindsay. "Nonprobative Photographs (Or Words) Inflate Truthiness." *Psychonomic Bulletin & Review*. October 2012.

76 Hilke Plassmann, John O'Doherty, Baba Shiv & Antonio Rangel. "Marketing Actions Can Modulate Neural Representations of Experienced Utility." *Proceedings of the National Academy of Sciences*. January 2008.

77 Matthieu Ricard, Antoine Lutz & Richard J. Davidson. "Mind of the Meditator." *Scientific American*. November 2014.

78 Frank R. Kardes & Bob M. Fennis. "The Role of the Need for Cognitive Closure in the Effectiveness of the Disrupt-then-Reframe Influence Technique." *Journal of Consumer Research.* October 2007.

79 Lan Jiang, Joandrea Hoegg, Darren W. Dahl & Amitava Chattopadhyay. "The Persuasive Role of Incidental Similarity on Attitudes and Purchase Intentions in a Sales Context." *Journal of Consumer Research.* February 2010.

80 Aner Sela, S. Christian Wheeler & Gülen Sarial-Abi. "'We' Are Not the Same as 'You and I': Causal Effects of Minor Language Variations on Consumers' Attitudes Toward Brands." *Journal of Consumer Research.* October 2012.

81 Praveen K. Kopalle, Donald R. Lehmann & John U. Farley. "Consumer Expectations and Culture: The Effect of Belief in Karma in India." *Journal of Consumer Research.* August 2010.

82 Keisha M. Cutright. "The Beauty of Boundaries: When and Why We Seek Structure in Consumption." *Journal of Consumer Research.* February 2012.

83 Juliano Laran, Amy N. Dalton & Eduardo B. Andrade. "Why Consumers Rebel Against Slogans." *Harvard Business Review.* November 2011.

84 Manoj Thomas & Claire I. Tsai. "Psychological Distance and Subjective Experience: How Distancing Reduces the Feeling of Difficulty." *Journal of Consumer Research.* August 2012.

85 Aparna A. Labroo & Jesper Nielsen. "Half the Thrill Is in the Chase: Twisted Inferences from Embodied Cognitions." *Journal of Consumer Research.* June 2010.

86 Ann Kronrod, Amir Grinstein & Luc Wathieu. "Enjoy! Hedonic Consumption and Compliance with Assertive Messages." *Journal of Consumer Research.* June 2012.

87 Vanessa M. Patrick & Henrik Hagtvedt. "'I Don't' Versus 'I Can't': When Empowered Refusal Motivates Goal-Directed Behavior." *Journal of Consumer Research.* August 2012.

88 Niro Sivanathan and Nathan Petit. "Protecting the Self Through Consumption: Status Goods as Affirmational Commodities." *Journal of Experimental Social Psychology.* May 2010.

89 Rosellina Ferraro, Baba Shiv & James R. Bettman. "Let Us Eat and Drink, for Tomorrow We Shall Die: Effects of Mortality Salience and Self-Esteem on Self-Regulation in Consumer Choice." *Journal of Consumer Research*. June 2005.

90 Liat Hadar, Sanjay Sood & Craig R. Fox. "Subjective Knowledge in Consumer Financial Decisions." *Journal of Marketing Research*. June 2013.

91 Jonathan Levav, Nicholas Reinholtz & Claire Lin. "The Effect of Ordering Decisions by Choice-Set Size on Consumer Search." *Journal of Consumer Research*. October 2012.

92 Risto Moisio, Eric J. Arnould & James W. Gentry. "Productive Consumption in the Class-Mediated Construction of Domestic Masculinity: Do-It-Yourself (DIY) Home Improvement in Men's Identity Work." *Journal of Consumer Research*. August 2013.

93 Katherine White & Jennifer J. Argo. "When Imitation Doesn't Flatter: The Role of Consumer Distinctiveness in Responses to Mimicry." *Journal of Consumer Research*. December 2011.

94 Pascale Quester & Alexandre Steyer. "Revisiting Individual Choices in Group Settings: The Long and Winding (Less-Traveled) Road." *Journal of Consumer Research*. April 2010.

95 Xun (Irene) Huang, Ping Dong & Anirban Mukhopadhyay. "Proud to Belong or Proudly Different? Lay Theories Determine Contrasting Effects of Incidental Pride on Uniqueness Seeking." *Journal of Consumer Research*. October 2014.

96 Sheena S. Iyengar & Mark R. Lepper. "When Choice Is Demotivating: Can One Desire Too Much of a Good Thing?" *Journal of Personality and Social Psychology*. December 2000.

97 Jinhee Choi & Ayelet Fishbach. "Choice as an End Versus a Means." *Journal of Marketing Research*. June 2011.

98 Joseph K. Goodman & Selin A. Malkoc. "Choosing for the Here and Now Versus There and Later: The Moderating Role of Psychological Distance on Assortment Size Preference." *Journal of Consumer Research*. December 2012.

99 Anne-Laure Sellier & Darren W Dahl. "Focus! Creative Success Is Enjoyed Through Restricted Choice." *Journal of Marketing Research*. December 2011.

100 Dirk Smeesters & Naomi Mandel. "Positive and Negative Media Image Effects on the Self." *Journal of Consumer Research*. March 2006.

101 Edith Shalev & Vicki G. Morwitz. "Influence via Comparison-Driven Self Evaluation and Restoration: The Case of the Low-Status Influencer." *Journal of Consumer Research*. February 2012.

102 Katherine E. Loveland, Dirk Smeesters & Naomi Mandel. "Still Preoccupied with 1995: The Need to Belong and Preference for Nostalgic Products." *Journal of Consumer Research*. October 2010.

103 Sigurd Villads Troye & Magne Supphellen. "Consumer Participation in Coproduction: 'I Made It Myself' Effects on Consumers' Sensory Perceptions and Evaluations of Outcome and Input Product." *Journal of Marketing*. March 2012.

104 Michel Tuan Pham, Caroline Goukens, Donald R. Lehmann & Jennifer Ames Stuart. "Shaping Customer Satisfaction Through Self-Awareness Cues." *Journal of Marketing Research*. October 2010.

105 Didem Kurt & J. Jeffrey Inman. "Mispredicting Others' Valuations: Self-Other Difference in the Context of Endowment." *Journal of Consumer Research*. June 2013.

106 Pankaj Aggarwal & Meng Zhang. "The Moderating Effect of Relationship Norm Salience on Consumers' Loss Aversion." *Journal of Consumer Research*. December 2006.

107 Jerry M. Burger & David F. Caldwell. "When Opportunity Knocks: The Effect of a Perceived Unique Opportunity on Compliance." *Group Processes & Intergroup Relations*. September 2011.

108 Rajkumar Venkatesan & Paul W. Farris. "Measuring and Managing Returns from Retailer-Customized Coupon Campaigns." *Journal of Marketing*. January 2012.

109 Christian Homburg, Nicole Koschate & Wayne D. Hoyer. "Do Satisfied Customers Really Pay More? A Study of the Relationship Between Customer Satisfaction and Willingness to Pay." *Journal of Marketing*. April 2005.

110 Devavrat Purohit & Joydeep Srivastava. "Effect of Manufacturer Reputation, Retailer Reputation, and Product Warranty on Consumer Judgments of Product Quality: A Cue Diagnosticity Framework." *Journal of Consumer Psychology*. 10(3). 2001.

111 Barry Schwartz, Andrew Ward, John Monterosso, Sonja Lyubomirsky, Katherine White & Darrin R. Lehman. "Maximizing Versus Satisficing: Happiness Is a Matter of Choice." *Journal of Personality and Social Psychology*. November 2002.

112 Deniz Ucbasaran, Paul Westhead & Mike Wright. "Why Serial Entrepreneurs Don't Learn from Failure." *Harvard Business Review*. April 2011.

113 A. Gandomi & S. Zolfaghari. "A Stochastic Model on the Profitability of Loyalty Programs." *Computers & Industrial Engineering*. April 2011.

114 Carl Senior, Robin Martin, Michael West & Rowena M. Yeats. "How Earlobes Can Signify Leadership Potential." *Harvard Business Review*. November 2011.

115 Brian R. Kinard & Jerry L. Kinard. "The Effect of Receipt Personalization on Tipping Behavior." *Journal of Consumer Behaviour*. July/August 2013.

116 Arch G. Woodside, Suresh Sood & Kenneth E. Miller. "When Consumers and Brands Talk: Storytelling Theory and Research in Psychology and Marketing." *Psychology & Marketing*. February 2008.

117 Joandrea Hoegg & Michael V. Lewis. "The Impact of Candidate Appearance and Advertising Strategies on Election Results." *Journal of Marketing Research*. October 2011.

118 Hajo Adam & Adam D. Galinsky. "Enclothed Cognition." *Journal of Experimental Social Psychology*. July 2012.

119 Alexander Haas & Peter Kenning. "Utilitarian and Hedonic Motivators of Shoppers' Decision to Consult with Salespeople." *Journal of Retailing*. September 2014.

120 Derek R. Avery, Patrick F. McKay, Scott Tonidandel, Sabrina D. Volpone & Mark A. Morris. "Is There Method to the Madness? Examining How Racioethnic Matching Influences Retail Store Productivity." *Personnel Psychology*. Spring 2012.

121 Jennifer J. Argo & Kelley J. Main. "Stigma-by-Association in Coupon Redemption: Looking Cheap Because of Others." *Journal of Consumer Research*. December 2008.

122 Brent A. Scott & Timothy A. Judge. "Beauty, Personality, and Affect as Antecedents of Counterproductive Work Behavior Receipt." *Human Performance*. 26(2). 2013.

123 Ben Dattner & Robert Hogan. "Managing Yourself: Can You Handle Failure?" *Harvard Business Review*. April 2011.

124 Ronald Burns, Patrick Kinkade & Michael Bachmann. "Getting Hosed: Petty Theft in the Car Wash Industry and the Fifth Suitability Criterion in Routine Activities Theory." *The Social Science Journal*. September 2012.

125 Christine Porath, Debbie MacInnis & Valerie Folkes. "Witnessing Incivility Among Employees: Effects on Consumer Anger and Negative Inferences About Companies." *Journal of Consumer Research*. August 2010.

126 Anja Reimer & Valerie Folkes. "Consumers' Inferences About Quality Across Diverse Service Providers." *Psychology & Marketing*. November 2009.

Index

Index

Index

Made in the USA
San Bernardino, CA
04 February 2015